EXPLORING THE SUBCONSCIOUS
USING NEW TECHNOLOGY

CMC Ltd.

About the Author

Gwyn Hocking has been interested in novel ways of exploring the subconscious for the last 20 years and has researched the subject extensively.

He was attracted by some of the scientific paranormal phenomena such as the reported extra sensory perceptions (ESP) observations of the structures of atoms and molecules and the Uri Geller ESP experiments at Stanford University.

He has written many papers on the subject of ESP and has lectured intensively on the subject.

As a Scientist, Senior Lecturer and Reader at the University of London he is able to understand the intricacies and patterns of electronic signal both applied to and emitted by the brain and has aimed to bring this subject to the reader in a simple and entertaining way. The experiences of many eminent people are narrated in the context of brainwave activity and its effect on visualisation and creativity. The author takes us through his experiences on an exploration mission to the subconscious and gives us examples of how music, light and sound, sensory deprivation etc. can affect our brain and performance.

EXPLORING THE SUBCONSCIOUS
USING NEW TECHNOLOGY

M.G. Hocking Ph.D.

To
C. Maxwell Cade & Geoffrey Blundell
Pioneers in Biofeedback

Hocking, M.G.,

....

First edition, first print, published April 1993

ISBN 0 9521099 0 5

Mind Explorer Series:
Published by CMC LTD.
25 Lexham Gardens,
London W8 5JJ
UK
Tel. 071-581 9919 Fax. 071-225 8712

Acknowledgements

I would like to thank my wife for her understanding during the writing of this book. I am also indebted to Dr V. Vasantasree for reading the proof of this manuscript and for her suggestions. My thanks also go to Dr Paulette Sidky for editing and publishing the book.

CONTENTS

List of Figures

PREFACE

VISUALISATION

From time immemorial, visualisation seems to always have been the prerogative of a few artists or advanced meditators. For the average person, dreams were his only source of visual creativity.

The mingling of science and art can be seen in the inspired paintings, sculptures and inventions of Leonardo Da Vinci and Michael Angelo (The Creation in Rome and David statue in Florence).

But with the industrial revolution, further separation of the two occurred; logic and analysis took dominance. As we progress and modernise our world, this gap leaves us empty and isolated from our inner being. We probe for ways to "find" ourselves.

Yoga, meditation, chanting etc. are prescribed but in our busy lives, our progress seems slow. Sceptics cannot see reason or link between modern living and ancient rituals. Scientists and engineers see no meeting of paths between their analytical thinking and esoteric or intangible dreams. A few investigators however have tried to understand what lies beyond our obvious abilities. Today, major advances in electronics development has placed at our disposal a range of sophisticated techniques which we can use to examine ourselves and our brains in order to understand why the process of visualisation occurs more readily for some than for others.

The understanding of our brain rhythms and how these are affected by our state of visualisation, relaxation or thinking etc. was the corner stone of further development. With this knowledge we are now able to use electronic equipments to guide our brain rhythms so that we can achieve any desired brain-state. These techniques speed the process of visualisation, creativity, meditation, relaxation etc. which take far longer by traditional means.

This book aims to explain these new techniques and the processes involved. Chapter 1 deals with creativity and gives examples of famous scientists who were able to combine visualisation with inventive and thinking ability. A discussion of what could lie beyond our five senses spurs us to try to understand more about ourselves. Chapter 2 gives us the background and explains our brain activity and how this can be scientifically measured. This is done in simple layman's language for accessibility. Chapter 3 follows and explains the different functions of both our right and left brain hemispheres and the possibility of activating the right hemisphere to increase our creative abilities; most of us have a dominant left brain activity of logic and deduction. The enhancement of right brain activity would therefore add a new dimension to our performance. Mind training is therefore very important and this is covered in chapter 4. Various traditional meditation techniques are presented and their role in increasing visualisation is discussed. Chapter 5 discusses the effects of drugs etc. in relation to our natural physiological production of endorphins. The use of the various instruments (to be discussed in later chapters) is shown to be effective in reducing depression and has been demonstrated as an aid to alleviating drug withdrawal symptoms. Chapter 6 defines the term "Biofeedback" and illustrates how by simply imagining or visualising a change in our state, we can actually change it. For example imagining ourselves to be colder or warmer or more relaxed etc. will actually induce the real change. Chapter 7 onwards describes the various electronic equipment available on the market which can be used to help us in achieving relaxation, meditation, creativity, memory etc. Light and sound technology is described and we see how simple walkman size devices (fun and easy to use) can be used to synchronise our left and right brain hemispheres and how we can induce various states by the push of a button. Chapter 8 deals with electro-encephalograph (EEG) units which can be used to monitor the changes in our brain rhythms as we perform various tasks and how these can be used in conjunction with biofeedback, to aid us along the path. Exercises are given to illustrate the various effects. A journey for the mind is described (pathworking) in chapter 9. Chapter 10 describes flotation tanks and how these can be used to bring up the subconscious simply by removing sensory input from our five senses. Relaxation and drug-free imagery are immediate results. Finally Chapter 11 describes other useful machines such as the cranial electrical stimulator (CES) which can be used to reduce pain by increasing our endorphin production. Ganzfeld (entire field) units are used to remove thoughts from our mind and help us relax. Finally, dream machines are used to make us self-conscious and aware in our dreams, so that we are able to guide them and remember them.

The material in this book has been extensively researched as evidenced by the large number of references which the reader can see for further information. Scientific data (described simply) is used to shed light on our behaviour and state of being and to elucidate how this relates to our brain activity.

Training of the mind to bring out our latent creative abilities and balancing our logical minds is now an accepted concept by businessmen, sportsmen and even the US army as a means of improved performance. The techniques described in this book are now extensively used in the USA and increasing in Europe.

This book is a necessary guide for anyone interested in reducing stress, insomnia, etc. or increasing their creativity, inventive ability, learning skills etc., or exploring the subconscious through easier entry to meditative states. It is a necessary guide for anyone contemplating the use of any of the techniques.

"The normal waking state is neither the highest nor the most effective state of which the human mind is capable. There are states of vastly greater awareness which one can enter briefly and then return to normal living, enriched, enlivened and enhanced." - C. Maxwell Cade & N. Coxhead.

"Then only is our life a whole, when action and contemplation dwell in us side by side, and we are perfectly in both of them at once."
- Jan van Ruysbroeck.

CHAPTER 1

CONSCIOUSNESS- THE ULTIMATE FRONTIER

"Let us learn to dream, gentlemen": Kekulé (a famous chemist)

A study of creative scientists (27) says, "Creative persons appear to have stumbled onto and then developed to a high degree of perfection the ability to visualise ... in the area in which they are creative. This is illustrated by reports by many of the great inventors of the past."

The mathematician Poincare described a relaxed condition in which mathematical ideas *"rose in clouds, dancing before him and colliding and combining"* into what he recognised as the first set of Fuchsian Functions, the solution to a problem he had been trying to solve.

The chemist Kekulé spoke of deep dreamlike reveries, leading to his theory of molecular constitution, "I turned my chair to the fire and dozed. Again the atoms were gambolling before my eyes. My mental eye, rendered more acute by repeated visions of this kind, could now distinguish larger structures, in manifold conformation; long rows, sometimes closely fitted together, all twisting in snakelike motion. One of the snakes seized hold of its own tail and the form whiled mockingly before my eyes. As if by a flash of lightening I awoke ..." He urged his contemporaries, "*Let us learn to dream, gentlemen.*"

Another scientist dreamed a sought-for formula, wakened, and hurriedly scribbled it down - only to find he could not read it the next morning! Each succeeding night he concentrated on re-dreaming it and eventually succeeded. This time he got up and carefully recorded the formula, for which he was awarded the Nobel Prize (28).

The author Jean Cocteau reports visualising, "*as if from a seat in a theatre, three acts in which appeared an epoch and characters about which I had no documentary information*", which formed his subsequent play "The Knights of the Round Table". Robert Louis Stevenson's ability to command his mind to furnish him with a story while he slept is well documented. There are many other such accounts, e.g. Graham Greene's ability to dream plots for his novels (110).

These accounts show that valuable ideas may lie dormant in the deeper and less accessible parts of the mind.

Beyond our 5 Senses:

Beyond our normal 5 senses there is evidence that we have other faculties which are normally subliminal and thus not perceived (1-25;32-42;45-47;84-105;111;113-116;123). These faculties may be responsible for intuitions which are translated into all kinds of vitally important creative work, ranging from scientific and engineering invention to the composing of great music and art. Also, greatly enhanced and fast learning rates may be achieved, with no wandering of attention and no boredom, if the mind is placed in certain special states. It is thus very worthwhile to explore this subliminal region of the mind. There is also evidence that if the mind is deprived of sensory input, it "turns up the volume control" and in this state its normally subliminal and subconscious regions can be perceived.

Many traditional methods (14,15) exist for this purpose, many of them in the monastic traditions of all religions, but the process is in no way tied to any religion or belief and can be performed in an entirely secular way, as I shall show below. Science has recently moved into this fascinating field and has evolved various electronic units which greatly assist this quest. Before reviewing these units it is necessary to give some background against which they can easily be understood.

Many years ago I met Maharishi Mahesh Yogi (the guru of the Beatles and founder of 'Transcendental Meditation' or TM). In describing his method of approaching the subliminal areas of the mind he told me to repeat a short word after him; he then spoke this word for me at (I estimate) about 4 or 5 repetitions per second. At the time I thought this was surprisingly fast; I would have expected a slow rate of about 1 per second. Many years later, I discovered why he chose that rate - it is the rate of a particular electrical frequency in the brain called theta waves. It doesn't matter much what the repeated word is; a purely secular word like "one" can be used and is equally effective. A long line of Hindu monks have been using this method from time immemorial and it must have evolved because it works and not (perhaps) because they knew the theta frequency was the right one to chose. It may take years to achieve results by this traditional method, trying verbally to "drive" the brain at the theta frequency; but electronic light and sound units are now available which may achieve this result in minutes! This has been called a form of 'instant mysticism'.

Another way to modify brainwaves is by drugs (1,6,20). This is also a form of instant mysticism, but usually the people involved are wrongly motivated and the flaws in one's personality can be magnified a thousand fold and reflected back at one, unless proper preparation is made. The personality may disintegrate, opposite to the other methods to be described below.

Modern biofeedback methods for revealing the inaccessible regions of the mind are an important area for investigation and training. The deeper levels of the mind are the source of all kinds of vitally important creative work. Later some electronic units will be described, which allow us to become self-conscious and aware during a dream.

Retrieval of 'twilight-state' material can be facilitated by speaking, into a running tape-recorder, just one word which will later act as a powerful mnemonic to recover the rest later. Attempts to give a complete story while in the twilight state will usually end it abruptly.

Most people live at a lesser efficiency than they are actually capable of. A few people, like Edison and Einstein, have a natural ability (or have chanced across how to develop it) for excellent performance. But following recent advances in electronics this can now be learnt and we do not any longer have to just admire genius in others: we can create it in ourselves.

Whatever your day time activity, you can benefit from the electronic units described in this book. We are fortunate in living in an age of great electronic advances.

Another aspect is the attainment of mystical states, which allow insights into depths of truth unattainable by the discursive intellect. Such insights have a tremendous sense of authority (45).

Koestler (125) writes, "... *the temporary relinquishing of conscious controls liberates the mind from certain constraints which are necessary to maintain the disciplined routine of thoughts but may become an impediment to the creative leap; at the same time other types of ideation on more primitive levels of mental organisation are brought into activity.*"

Before proceeding further, it is necessary to give some basic information about the brain.

CHAPTER 2

BRAIN ACTIVITY

In Meditation, you don't work with the "Mind", you work with "Awareness"

During the normal working of the brain, very small electrical signals are generated in it. These can be detected and displayed using an electronic amplifier (electro-encephalograph, EEG). These signals were first discovered about 100 years ago. Alternating low frequency voltages of about 10 microvolts amplitude were detected on the scalp and recorded by a sensitive galvanometer. Today we use amplifiers to magnify these voltages. Over a million miles of EEG chart paper have been used in the last half century! So EEG instrumentation is clearly well established.

A few gifted individuals in our society have made outstanding contributions to science and the arts. In case a clue to this might lie in their brain electrical activity, some of these people were investigated using an EEG. An explanation is necessary about the different types of electrical signals in the brain, which are best classified by their frequency [Fig. 1].

Relation of Electrical Signals in the Brain to our State:

BETA (around 20 cycles per second or Hz) is our normal everyday thinking state. [There are also higher frequencies, such as those around 400 cycles per second, called P1 & P2].

ALPHA (around 10 Hz) is our state with eyes closed and all thoughts excluded from the mind, and is fairly easy to achieve. Any attempt at thinking will immediately put us back into a beta state again. But it is possible to LEARN how to think in the alpha state and even to solve problems while in it. A few gifted individuals were discovered to have this ability naturally, e.g. the famous physicist Albert Einstein was found to able to think about problems while in an alpha state. This state borders on the next-lower state, the theta state (about 6 Hz), which is thought to be responsible for the creative and intuitive faculties. So the alpha state is the doorway to the theta state, whereas the everyday beta state is 'once-removed' from it. Einstein thought in images, not words:
"Imagination is more important than knowledge." - A. Einstein.

Edison used to relax in a chair with a metal sheet on the floor and a rubber ball in his hand over it; relaxation produces the alpha state and the deeper intuitive theta state, but this is usually accompanied by loss of the beta which means one falls asleep. Edison prevented this happening because the ball then fell on the sheet which woke him up and in this way he maintained some activity in beta, alpha and theta and was able to bring the inventions of this special state into his aware mind.

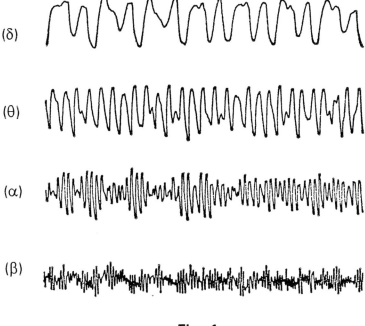

Fig. 1

Principal Brain Rhythms found in EEGs

(From top to bottom)

(δ)	Delta	= 0.5	to 3.5	cycles per second.
(θ)	Theta	= 4	to 7	cycles per second.
(α)	Alpha	= 8	to 13	cycles per second.
(β)	Beta	= 14	to 30	cycles per second.

9

A monotonous job can induce an alpha state, e.g. driving a car on a long journey. Car makers have devised an alpha meter alarm for drivers to wear, with a simple headband. An alternative method is an "eyes closed" detector which sounds an alarm if the eyes stay closed for more than a preset short time.

Opening the eyes makes alpha hard to produce for beginners. But if you open your eyes disinterstedly, i.e. without seeing anything, just gazing abstractly, then with practice you can produce alpha waves. Alpha by itself is no good - you must produce alpha with some beta and theta as well, the theta for contacting the subliminal levels of the mind (inner experience) and the beta as a link to normal consciousness.

THETA (around 6 Hz) is our state when dreaming. It is a state of visual imagery which a very few gifted individuals are able to enter spontaneously at will. A traditional monastic exercise in advanced meditation is to cup one's hands and see (with visual imagery) a daffodil in one's hands. Success in this traditional meditation (mind training) method is normally many years away, but with EEG biofeedback or the use of an electronic light and sound unit or similar, success is only hours away and one can even learn fairly quickly to develop the state of mind needed to reach theta wave production by the brain without having to use the machines. Theta is a mind state for problem solving and entry to it is a worthwhile pursuit.

It is useless to CONCENTRATE (a left brain hemisphere activity - explained in Chapter 3) on producing a daffodil image, or any other meditation imagery exercise. One has to IMAGINE it only (i.e. use the right brain hemisphere). And when it appears, one has to be an entirely DISINTERESTED observer, or it will vanish just like a dream vanishes if you try to analyse it while it is going on. It is a knack to observe a daffodil or a dream state vision in a disinterested way. To continue in a theta state, it is essential to develop this knack. Any attempt to think about (analyse) the scene will instantly destroy it. The brain reverts back to its everyday beta state. With continued practice the above-mentioned knack can be cultivated.

The right (artistic) hemisphere of the brain generates visual images. The left (analytical) hemisphere does not. **In meditation, you don't work with the "mind", you work with "awareness"**. 'Meditation' is a secular word, merely meaning a form of mind training. See Chapter 4.

Kasamatsu & Hirai (29) studied the brainwave output from people with long traditional training in mind control and found a shift from beta through alpha to theta waves, which the people producing the waves described as a state of "knowing" (= right hemisphere) rather than of "thinking" (= left hemisphere). Years of training are required unless light & sound machines or biofeedback equipment etc is available. These will be described later in this book.

A brain in a theta state is in a state of visual imagery and because of the unusual luminous quality of the images this state was termed, in mediaeval times, the astral state. So-called astral consciousness is not something weird; it is NOTHING MORE than a state of visual imagery. This does not mean it is unreal; the image of the daffodil is absolutely as real and solid in its "region" as a wooden table is in our physical region, although an inability to distinguish the two is a good definition of insanity. Do not let this put you off, of course, but just remember when you see your daffodil that it is entirely astral and not physical. With (a lot of) practice, one can slip in and out of astral and physical vision without difficulty. It is a knack. A few individuals have this ability naturally; a famous one was William Blake.

The daffodil is no greater illusion than a physical table, because the table can be made from materials found available in the physical world just as the the daffodil can be made from the materials of the astral level. Both are thus equally **constructs** and both are thus equally illusory!

Children's brainwaves are normally rich in theta, which links with their imaginative and special type of consciousness, which unfortunately leaves us as we grow up. But it can be regained by EEG theta training, for example. Children's imaginary playing is akin to what is called pathworking (23). In the theta state our consciousness has become transferred to a so-called astral level. A theta state is a state of visual imagery and with (a lot of) training one can enter this without falling asleep and losing consciousness. This is one of the major uses of an EEG as a biofeedback device and of light and sound and other units.

DELTA is the fourth and last major brainwave rhythm, about 1 Hz, and is the state of dreamless sleep. (Theta is dreaming sleep). EEG studies have shown that a few people like psychic healers and other psychics can produce delta while in a normal conscious state. One of my colleagues can produce delta easily on request by "going very quiet". Delta is associated with psychic abilities. The pioneer mind-researcher Maxwell Cade has successfully used an EEG to identify potential trainees to be effective psychic healers. Maxwell Cade, using an EEG also showed that when a psychic healer TOUCHES a patient, the patient's EEG pattern becomes the same as that of the healer (the "laying on of hands"). There is no orthodox scientific explanation of this phenomenon. A meditation teacher with developed inner intuitive faculties can do the same - hence the value of meditating in the presence of a gifted teacher, but they are as rare as hen's teeth!

Iamblichus, in the third century, describes a state between waking & sleeping in which voices are heard and sometimes "a bright & tranquil light shines forth". More well-known are Swedenborg's writings about his 'distant vision' and other experiences and ways of inducing them (123).

CHAPTER 3

LEFT AND RIGHT BRAIN HEMISPHERES

It was discovered long ago that we have almost independent left and right brain hemispheres (43, 127, 126). Oversimplifying for brevity, movements of the left hand are controlled by the right brain hemisphere and right hand movements by the left hemisphere. More recently it was discovered that the left brain hemisphere is the linear logical thinking part of the brain - a sort of calculator. About 2/3 of the population are left-brain dominant. In particular, technical people (e.g. scientists) are left-brain dominant. The right hemisphere is where visual imagery is perceived and so artists are right-brain dominant. The right hemisphere is responsible for spatial matters, like recognising faces, maps etc. and art appreciation, as well as music. In scientific people, the left brain is often so dominant that their right brains often close down & go to sleep because that hemisphere has nothing to do; they are literally 'half-asleep'

[Fig. 2]. Each brain hemisphere tends to be active and then dormant for some time, alternately, causing bouts of daydreaming while performing scientific calculations for example. In a recent interview, the celebrated Sri Satya Sai Baba commented that scientists have 'half-knowledge'. Ouspenski, a pupil of Gurdjieff (19), said, "*Man is asleep...life for him is only a dream...from which he never wakes.*" We are sleepwalkers moving about in a twilight of consciousness but believing ourselves to be awake (5).

This "half-asleep" condition of the brain is far from ideal because the right brain is thought to be the source of inspiration and intuition. So science and engineering which is done only with the left brain will be rather unimaginative, without inspiration or sparkle. If you want to bring inspiration to a technical activity, you need to activate the right brain, e.g. to invent a new process, or, if you are a business person, to run your business creatively.

Activating the Right Brain Hemisphere:

The right hemisphere is concerned with visual imagery and spatial perception, e.g. if you want to remember where you put a certain book, this recollection is done by the right brain. To activate it we need to look at a landscape for about half an hour; there must be no buildings in it or the left brain will start to analyse them! If you do a painting you will get better results if you paint with your left hand for a while because that hand is controlled by the right (artistic) brain.

Or instead, looking at a geometrical design, traditionally a mandala as shown in Fig. 3, will activate the right brain as follows:

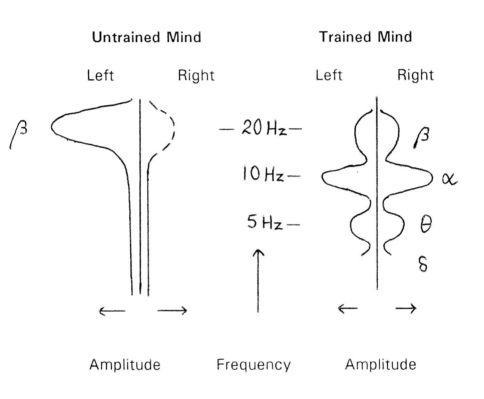

Fig. 2

Electro-encelograph (EEG) Patterns

Focus on the centre of the mandala (Fig. 3) and relax. After 5 minutes a quieting of the mind will begin to replace the mind's usual inner dialogue. After several sessions, extraneous thoughts etc. will be unable to penetrate into your consciousness. Prevent the left brain from trying to logically analyse the mandala, by keeping concentrating on its centre. At first you will find yourself looking for and analysing any geometrical symmetries which are present, but this is a logical-left-brain activity and should be ignored (just let the left brain get on with it). The next thing you will notice is probably boredom; this is the left brain having exhausted its logical analysis that is now trying to tempt you to give it up and do something else which it prefers! It is an activation barrier and if you persist you can get over it and activate the spatial domain of the right brain and the left brain begins to go to sleep. You then enter a slightly altered state of consciousness in which there is no feeling of boredom at all. In fact the bored feeling that you pass through is a sign of success - boredom here is a welcome sign because it means the left brain is protesting that there's nothing for it to do! Persist and it will close down.

After relaxing the grip of the left hemisphere on your consciousness by use of a mandala or by biofeedback, etc., you are ready for meditation, or for pathworking (Chapter 9).

A professor of architecture uses mandalas and guided imagery before starting his architectural designs (48). He teaches his students to enter the right brain mode and imagine that they are walking through the building before starting their design.

Sport is mainly a right brain activity - an old (and unfair!) trick is to make your opponent activate his left brain, e.g. by shouting comments or questions requiring logical analysis. This can irrecoverably destroy his game.

Fig. 3

Mandala

Judging from the number of computer games which involve wizards and magic, there is an increase (perhaps subconscious!) in the subconscious - i.e. in the right brain area of operation.

There are many ways of activating the right-brain, like meditation, Zen, light and sound machines (discussed in Chapter 7), hemi-sync tapes (Chapter 7), cranial electrical stimulation (CES)(Chapter 11), narcotic drugs (not recommended) etc., and an easy way is to spend an hour in a flotation tank (Chapter 10).

Right vs Left Brain Activity:

A remarkable demonstration of how completely dominated by the left brain our culture is, is that patients have had their entire right brain hemisphere surgically removed, without their noticing the slightest change in awareness subsequently!

If you ask yourself a question such as, "what shall I do with my life?", and write the answer with your right hand and then with your left hand, you will probably get different answers! The right brain has a quite different view of life (48). Zdenek gives valuable exercises to bring forward and develop the right brain (48).

Different cultures may progress along mainly left or mainly right brain development. Culture is reflected in language, as the following examples (well known to linguists) show. Indo-European languages have an analytical (left brain) subject-predicate structure, e.g. "The stone fell down", but the totally different language structure of the indigenous North American Indians has a process structure (right brain) and the event in the above example would be expressed as, "It stoned down". The subject (stone) would be expressed as a process (a verb, it stoned).

Consequently, European culture has developed in a linear logical scientific way (left brain), while North American Indian culture has developed in a spatial process way (right brain) and has produced shamanistic insights which most Europeans lack. Some grasp of these can be obtained from the books by Carlos Castaneda (20).

Once we have advanced along the "European" left brain path, our growth will stop unless we add the totally different "Red Indian" (for example) right brain development. Only then will we become fully integrated. Developing along only either the one, or the other path, will leave us quite unbalanced, although we may not realise this until the very environment starts to protest, as is now happening (e.g. global warming, ozone layer hole, etc.) (30).

The "European" path is closer to the material world and so has given rise to material wealth, while the "Red Indian" path is not and so has not. This does not make it any less valid than the "European" path. We are suffering much more than we realise through not encompassing the "Red Indian" way; see the Hopi video "*Koyaanisqatsi*" on this topic (30).

Dominance by the left hemisphere is strongly reinforced by our system of education. At birth the hemispheres have equal powers, but work independently. In childhood, considerable right-brain activity occurs: imagination, intuition, musical, little sense of time. But at school these are rewarded by disapproval: daydreamers. Intuitive thinking is so disapproved of and so much a right-brain activity that a recent study showed no correlation with examination grades: intuitive thinking is unrelated to college grades (51). But all recognised geniuses say their ideas have come from the unconscious, which can be identified with the right brain.

Balancing our Brain output:

Right-brain activity and theta brainwaves are needed for visual imagery. Light and sound machines and EEGs with biofeedback can fill both these requirements. The light and sound is applied to both hemispheres and this will wake up any dormancy in the right (or left) hemisphere. An EEG with biofeedback (e.g. displaying the brain activity on a screen) allows you to observe and it is possible with some practice to correct the pattern as desired.

After some use of the stroboscopic feature of a light and sound machine, there will be a lasting and beneficial tendency for both hemispheres to operate together. Another unit for equalising brainwave outputs is the alternophone (see also chapter 7); a note alternately played into left and right ears at an alternation frequency of about 4 Hz (the frequency with which the hemispheres naturally communicate via the corpus callosum) will produce a heightened state of consciousness after about 30 to 45 minutes (24). To activate the RAS (see Chapter 10), the sound pulses used in the alternophone must begin with a sharp crack - this relates to the cracking of a twig behind one which causes the primitive RAS to 'turn up' one's attention for a fight-or-flight response.

It has been reported that reverse speech is used by the right brain and hence if a tape recording of a conversation is played backwards, revealing words from the right brain can often be heard (126,127). Reverse-playing tape recorders are available to facilitate this.

Music is a right-brain activity and also removes stress. For those interested in the eastern tradition, listen to "Dorje Ling" by David Parsons (available from the publishers of this book). This has gongs, 12 foot Tibetan trumpets & deep bass Tibetan monastic voices. Listen with eyes closed to band 1 followed by band 4 only. It has a most remarkable effect; I have never heard anything like it.

For the western tradition, there are several choices. Movement 2 only (Et in terra pax) of Vivaldi's Gloria in D major (RV589) is unearthly in the rendering by the USSR Academy Chorus {film music of last 4 minutes of "Runaway Train" (now deleted except in USA, Milan CH067, CD)}, but not so striking in some other versions. Parts of "The Encircled Sea" by Boyle, "Spem in alium" by Tallis and Fantasia on a Theme by Thomas Tallis by Vaughan Williams are other recommended music. (Enquire from publishers of this book.) There are many other choices of music in the western tradition.

Music is further discussed at the end of the next chapter (Chapter 4). Poetry is also a right brain activity. To illustrate its effect read the poem at the end of this chapter. This remarkable poem is the result of right brain inspiration, albeit out of balance in this poet's case.

Phosphenes (after-images) have long been known to have special effects (24). Looking steadily at a 60 watt whitelight (mushroom) bulb at about 70 cm for 30 seconds creates a phosphene when the eyes are subsequently closed. Do not wear glasses while doing this; do not use the sun as a light source without precautions. An application in education in learning some formulae is to read them through and then review them mentally while looking at a phosphene in the dark. Some

French tests (24) report an increase in I.Q. by looking at phosphenes. The Roman emperor Julian was trained in the Greek Mysteries and shortly afterwards advised people to look at phosphenes, so we may perhaps infer that the use of phosphenes was taught in the Greek Mysteries. In the ancient Zoroastrian religion people were asked to look through a small opening at a fire, which would produce a phosphene (24). It is said that it increases one's insight or intuition.

To digress, the use of auguries in the Greek & Roman Mysteries is worth mentioning. Consider this: President Lincoln was killed in Ford's Theatre by a man who then ran to a warehouse. President Kennedy was killed in a Lincoln Continental car made by Ford, by a man in a warehouse belonging to Continental Warehouse Co, who then ran to a theatre. President Kennedy had a secretary called Lincoln, who advised him not to go to Dallas that day. President Lincoln had a secretary called Kennedy, who advised him not to go to the theatre. These are only some of the well-documented auguries surrounding President Kennedy's death.

Use of light and sound machines is also reported to increase I.Q., which until fairly recently was thought to be unchangeable for an individual throughout life (apart from its well-known variation with age). Two theories are that apprehension is reduced which allows higher I.Q. scores, but it has also been proposed that intelligence actually does increase: a beneficial increase in the number nerve connexions in the brain has been reported (2). Also a synchronicity of activity in the two hemispheres of the brain is reported for light and sound machines, hemisphere synchronising tapes and EEGs with bio-feedback. This effect gives a strong and beneficial enhancement of general brain power. Learning from pre-recorded tapes while simultaneously using these devices has been reported in several studies to be greatly enhanced (super learning) compared with normal learning (2). In the theta state the brain is capable of uncritical acceptance of information at about 3 times the normal rate. These mind machines are the technological equivalent of enriched environments which can stimulate brain growth and in minutes can produce an increase which takes a month to achieve in an ordinary environment (2).

Could we with ink the ocean fill,
Were every blade of grass a quill
And were the skies of parchment made
And every man a scribe by trade

To write the Love of God above
Would drain the ocean dry;
Nor could the scroll contain the whole,
Though stretched from Sky to Sky.

Author unknown

(found written on a wall in an asylum)

oo O oo

CHAPTER 4

MIND TRAINING

*"Meditation begins with the cessation of thought.
Thought is the cessation of meditation"   - Krishnamurti.*

*"One cannot see into the depths of a lake
unless the water surface is still & calm." -
Maharishi Mahesh Yogi.*

Mind training or meditation is provided as training courses (with outside teachers) by several multinational companies and even by the US Army.   This is partly because an important side benefit is the relief of stress; it is very important for a big company that its key executives are not off work due to stress-related conditions.   EEG patterns show stress as a large beta signal, usually on the left side only [Fig. 2, page 17].

Biofeedback:

Meditation can be greatly assisted by observing one's own brainwaves using an electro-encephalograph (EEG).   This is known as 'bio-feedback'. It can also be more conveniently assisted by using a light and sound machine which drives the brain frequency. The brain state required is that which has been observed in EEG studies on expert meditators, which is theta with some sidebands of alpha and beta as a link to consciousness (rather than to sleep) [Fig. 2, page 17].

Traditional Meditation Techniques:

Traditionally, meditation is taught by a teacher who purportedly has inner powers so that he or she is able to quickly correct the pupil's techniques because he can see the results of the pupils attempts at meditation on inner levels which are not accessible to ordinary people. This is correction by FEEDBACK of information. With a gifted teacher, inner illumination can be thus gained in a few months, which could take 10 or 20 years otherwise. Now an EEG can, to some extent, replace the teacher's inner powers and a light and sound machine can induce the desired brainwave pattern.

Meditation has been studied by several psychologists. Benson et al (73) studied traditional and modern systems (like 'Transcendental Meditation', TM) and biofeedback. They found that all systems worked by causing the relaxation response. From the commonalties of all the systems, they concluded that there are 4 preconditions for creating the relaxation response:

(i)   a steady stimulus, like a repeated word, or looking at a given object, which causes a shift from everyday logical thought;

(ii)   distractions must be ignored and attention returned to the meditation;

(iii)   decreased muscle activity is essential (comfortable position);

(iv)   quiet surroundings are essential.

To (iii) Maxwell Cade would add that the position must not be too comfortable or sleep occurs - a straight back avoids this (5). Use a chair with a firm back but not an armchair or you will fall asleep.   The traditional Indian lotus meditation position has this in mind.

Sadhu (14) has collected many excellent classic exercises on concentration and put them into a self-study practice course of graded difficulty.   E.g. look at a (mechanical) watch with a moving second hand and try to reach 2 minutes without any extraneous thoughts intruding;   concentrate only on the moving hand.   This is quite difficult for beginners, until the knack is obtained, and if a thought intrudes the 2-minute target time must start again!   Another exercise is to look at the head of a pin and concentrate only on it for a target time.   The next exercise requires 4 dimensions and so cannot be performed with the 3-dimensional normal way of thinking.

Some training in concentration is necessary, in normal conditions, at least the ability to exclude unwanted thoughts and quieten the mental dialogue.

But all 4 of the requisites (i) to (iv) listed above are immediately and effortlessly produced by flotation!   This is discussed in Chapter 10.   The traditional need for avoiding an over-comfortable position is also sidestepped in the tank because other (automatic) mechanisms (the Reticular Activating System, RAS, explained in Chapter 10) prevent sleep.

The problem with traditional meditation systems is that they are not easy, requiring considerable time & effort.   Many people give up.   A flotation tank provides the easiest system giving all the benefits obtainable by advanced meditation and its beneficial physical effects are not just temporary. It apparently makes the hypothalamus lastingly more stress resistant (59,79), without any particular conscious effort being directed to this end (41).

Mindfulness is a technique where full attention is given to the changing content of one's awareness, e.g. Zen meditation (5). In contrast, in concentrative meditation, one's whole attention is given to a particular idea, to reach absorption into it, e.g. Christian, Sufi and Yoga meditation systems.

You may create (or discover) an 'inner advisor'. This is a powerful technique and an outstanding book on it is reference (47).

Even people who have never experienced deep relaxation have it conferred on them in a flotation tank (discussed in Chapter 10), most usually in their first float (41).

Breathing Exercises:

Breathing exercises are very important and are discussed by Cade & Coxhead (5). They suggest full concentration on the breathing process only, excluding all else and not changing one's field of view, for 5-10 minutes. If you remain conscious of yourself, you cannot succeed. In time, a brief state is reached where sounds are not heard and no external world exists; one is lost in one's own mindfulness of breathing. Self-consciousness becomes identified with one's breathing and if the attention is held on it long enough, one becomes one with one's own breathing. Then the mind and body merge. In this brief state is joy, happiness & tranquillity but it takes repeated practice to extend its duration & lead to very high mystic achievements. The flotation tank (Chapter 10) makes the whole process very much easier.

Simple Breathing Exercise
A simple breathing exercise can activate the right side of the brain: alternate nostril breathing. Close your right nostril with the thumb and inhale to a count of 4 (say); hold your breath for a count of 4 and then breath out through your right nostril for a count of 4 (closing the left nostril with the forefinger); then hold your breath for a count of 4. Repeat this cycle many times until you notice a sense of clarity. This should be done daily. Meditation or an imagery exercise will also activate the right brain & balance the hemispheres. See references 48 & 126.

Sufi Breathing Exercise
The following advanced traditional breathing exercise will eventually take your consciousness aloft.

Place right-hand middle finger over right nostril and left thumb over left nostril.

Inhale via <u>left</u> nostril. Imagine current <u>rising</u> via <u>LHS</u> branch of spine + a <u>clockwise</u> spiralling force going <u>up</u>.
Then turn eyes up.

Exhale via <u>right</u> nostril. Imagine current <u>descending</u> via <u>RHS</u> branch of spine + a <u>clockwise</u> spiralling force going <u>down</u>.
Eyes normal.

Inhale via <u>right</u> nostril. Imagine current <u>rising</u> via <u>RHS</u> branch of spine + <u>anticlockwise</u> spiralling force going <u>up</u>.
Then turn eyes up.

Exhale via <u>left</u> nostril. Imagine current <u>descending</u> via <u>LHS</u>

branch of spine + <u>anticlockwise</u> spiralling force going <u>down</u>.
Eyes normal.

Inhale via <u>both</u> nostrils. Imagine current <u>rising</u> via <u>middle</u> of
spine + <u>double</u> <u>helix</u> force going <u>up</u>. Eventually this step takes
your consciousness aloft.
Then turn eyes up.

Exhale via <u>both</u> nostrils. Imagine current <u>descending</u> via <u>middle</u>
of spine + double helix force <u>descending</u>.

Keep repeating this cycle.

Visualisation

Cade (5) describes a simple 'hypnagogstat', reminiscent of
Edison's method, which is effective in holding consciousness
into the *theta* state of visual imagery. This is simply a buzzer
with a reverse-acting push button which is released if one falls
asleep, whereupon the buzzing wakes one up again! Another
simple method described by Tart (46) is to hold up ones forearm
when in bed, resting it on the elbow, so that it falls abruptly if
one falls asleep and this wakes one up.

A sports (basketball) study where one group practised, one
group visualised and one group did neither, found equal 23%
improvements in the first two groups (75)!   A terminal cancer
study where patients visualised white blood cells as a vast army
of valiant white knights on horseback or ravenous white dogs or
powerful polar bears tearing apart & devouring the cancer cells,
showed doubling of longevity compared to a control group, and
many 'spontaneous remissions' (complete recoveries) (41, 50).

Any imagery can be used; Hutchison reports one person visualising his heart as a big house, walking into it and repairing its rooms like a carpenter with hammer and nails and plaster! The effect is almost instant (41).

A study was made where specific immune system activities were tested and the subjects were then hypnotised and told to visualise an activity increase in these same specific parts. Subsequent tests showed that the activities of these parts had actually risen (41). Hutchison points out that results using just hypnosis can be surpassed using tank floating (discussed in Chapter 10)(41).

Longevity should be increased by tank flotation, but results on this are not yet available. An "age clock" exists in the hypothalamus and neurotransmitter chemicals output normally decreases with age (52).

As Hutchison points out (41), manipulation of mental imagery is an ancient method for marshalling inner energies for healing. Biofeedback research shows that visualisation is very effective for modifying any body process - e.g. migraine is alleviated by visualising the hands dipped into hot water (which actually increases the blood flow to them). Muscle tensions can be relieved when imagined as tightly twisted cloth becoming limp (41).

In a study where women were told to visualise a warm towel over their breasts, all such subjects showed significant breast size increase, averaging from 1.5 to 2 inches, with many of the women also reporting a simultaneous body weight loss (53-56)!

As Hutchison says, "what you 'see' is what you get!" (41).

Taylor reports studies showing that 'high imagers' are more relaxed, creative, mature and flexible, than 'low imagers', and that absence of imagery correlates with strong aversion to act on impulse (58).

People having extraordinary memories are gifted with mental imaging abilities.

People using flotation tanks (discussed in Chapter 10) have higher theta wave output and visualise better than non-floaters (41). Everyone has the potential to visualise & produce theta waves and can realise this with training (light and sound machines, hemisync tapes, flotation tank, etc.).

The flotation tank is unique in producing both deep relaxation and strong mental imagery (visualisation) spontaneously & without effort. See a further discussion of visualisation in Chapter 10.

Refer to Chapter 9 on pathworking.

Music and Visualisation:

Music is a valuable help in visualisation, very well discussed by Drury (84).

A recent survey of 60 people who have had near-death experiences report hearing similar music to each other, which has a "beautiful floating sound and evokes feelings of overwhelming bliss" (116). Near-death experiences are reviewed by Moody and others (95-99). These people's hearts had temporarily stopped and in the survey afterwards music was played to them to discover which sounded most like the music they had heard while 'dead'. It was decisively New Age type synthesiser music and many of the survivors wept on hearing it again.

The highest ranking music was 'The Angels of Comfort' from 'Angelic Music' by Iasos (available from CMC) & other fairly high scorers are 'An Ending' from 'Apollo' by Brian Eno (available from CMC), 'Journey to Stratos' by John Serrie, 'Structures of Silence' by S. Roach and Neptune from the Planets Suite by G. Holst.

CHAPTER 5

DRUGS, NARCOTICS, OPIATES
vs
Our Natural ENDORPHIN Production

Drug misuse is an increasing problem in our society.

Brain cells contain receptor sites for opiates, called opiate receptors. If opiates (heroin, morphine, opium, methadone, etc.) are taken, they go to these sites and they also suppress the natural opiates (endorphins = "endogenous morphine" - i.e. internally produced morphine) which the body produces. Endorphin production thenafter continues to be much reduced, even for months after the opiate-taking is stopped. This gives withdrawal symptoms, because endorphins are needed to make one feel 'normal' and so if reduced, one feels 'ill' = withdrawal symptoms.

To summarise this, endorphins are the body's natural narcotics, which make us feel 'normal' by counteracting various depressive effects. Narcotic drugs inhibit endorphin production (and the receptor centres for them) and unpleasant withdrawal symptoms occur because the (natural) endorphins are absent and so nothing counteracts certain natural depressive effects which exist in our makeup. Some people have more, or have less, endorphin production and receptor centres, causing them to be happy, or depressive, types (59). This can however be beneficially modified by one or more of the techniques decried in later chapters. (Light & Sound, chapter 7, CES, chapter 11, and Flotation, chapter 10). These techniques increase endorphin production and can also increase one's immune system by increased control of hormone production (41).

Endorphins may be related to an area in the hypothalamus called a pleasure centre, which when stimulated electrically, gives intense pleasure such that all other activities will be dropped in its favour (60, 61)!

Endorphins and their generation:

Endorphin levels are naturally (automatically) increased within the brain, to cause a mild euphoria either as a reward for doing something which the body "considers" beneficial (e.g. eating, smoking etc.), or, to ease pain (e.g. endorphins are released after about 40 minutes of running - causing what is called "the runner's high"). Runners can feel (mild) withdrawal symptoms if they miss a habitual running session. This euphoric release of endorphins by low to moderate levels of pain also gives a rational explanation for other, non-beneficial, activities like masochism which are otherwise bizarre.

Endorphins also explain the pain-killing mechanism of acupuncture needles when these are used for anaesthesia, from the following experiment: Naloxone is a synthetic drug of opiate structure but is without the pain-killing or euphoric effects of the opiates. It thus uselessly blocks up the opiate receptors. Anaesthesia by acupuncture will not work if Naloxone was pre-administered, proving that acupuncture anaesthesia is due to endorphin release by the acupuncture needle (62-64).

Techniques to enhance Endorphin production:

<u>Cranial electrical stimulation</u> (CES) also causes endorphin release & consequent pain relief & euphoria. Depression or unhappiness can be alleviated if we can enhance endorphin production. <u>Floating</u> is also analgesic and euphoric. In addition, in the tank environment, the RAS (Reticular Activating System in the brain - explained in Chapter 10) switches awareness away from the body, where nothing is happening, to the mind; all pain consequently fades away. Further, the tank distorts (shortens) time perception and this effect is analgesic.

After a 30 minute alpha frequency session with a <u>light & sound machine</u>, Cady & Shealy (124) found a 25% rise in endorphin level, 21% rise in serotonin and 11% rise in norepinephrin, by blood tests on 11 people in good health. An increased feeling of well-being was generated.

Endorphins determine what the world "looks like" for each of us, by selectively filtering (via an anciently evolved inherited filter) every sense input before passing it to our higher levels of consciousness: no-one really knows what the world looks like, as the philosophers Berkeley & Hume had earlier realised. Our impressions of it as a child are also, and significantly, different from those we have now.

Addiction is not confined to narcotic drugs. Alcohol is addictive because it causes the brain to release endorphins. Such addiction (releasing endorphins) can also involve cigarettes, food, work, coffee, sex, gambling, buying, running, religion, and all flow activities and basic human drives and anything involving the body's reward system, described above (57). Overeating leading to obesity is due to the depletion, every few hours, of the pleasure chemicals, such that withdrawal symptoms appear. The same pattern applies to the other activities listed above. One activity can compensate for lack of another.

Floating is the (effortless) answer to these addictions, without, apparently, itself being also an addiction!

Meditation (non-tank) as might be expected, also causes a dramatic reduction in addictions (65-67), but it requires some continuing effort.

Valium, Librium and benzodiazepine drugs relieve anxiety by fitting into what are (anachronistically!) termed 'valium receptors' in the brain (anciently evolved and so obviously not intended for the synthetic drug Valium, but for a natural anti-anxiety substance). Use of Valium is thus addictive, similarly to opiates. Valium is also probably dangerous, being linked to breast cancer in one study (68).

Behavioural science studies reveal that doing things we enjoy doing, apparently provides an intrinsic reward and has been called a "flow experience", "a holistic sensation that people feel when they act with total involvement" (69). An even match is needed between a challenge and a person's ability to meet it, to avoid the two extremes of either boredom (no challenge) or anxiety (overwhelming challenge) and obtain enjoyment. Challenges which constitute flow experiences may be predominantly physical, like rock climbing or sailing, or mental like playing chess. Hutchison describes tank floating (described in Chapter 10) as a flow experience, one reason being that the tank is both experience and environment (41). The chess player must find the equally matched opponent, but the tank floater always finds in the tank a perfect match! The tank eliminates both boredom & anxiety; the mind stays very alert which counteracts all boredom by immersing us profoundly in our awareness (41).

'Flow' is difficult to maintain for long in the real world, as things are usually beyond our control there (69). But the feeling of control, developed in the tank, can be carried forward into the outside world.

Drug abuse

Light & sound machines have been used to alleviate withdrawal symptoms, if daily sessions are used, especially at theta frequencies. Cranial electrical stimulators (CES machines) are reported to be very effective for treatment of withdrawal and to help prevent further drug misuse. Similarly flotation as discussed previously (41).

Psychedelic Drugs

This is beyond the intended scope of this book. The remarkable effects of these drugs, taken under controlled conditions in a supportive clinical surrounding, are well documented (1, 6, 85-89). Dangerous side effects can ensue if taken without clinical supervision.

CHAPTER 6

BIOFEEDBACK

In biofeedback, a display or meter is viewed by the subject and shows one or more of his/her body parameters (such as temperature, brainwave pattern etc.). It has been found that the subject is then able to alter this parameter through biofeedback making this a very powerful tool to alter one's state.

As an example of biofeedback, Maxwell Cade (5) reports that if a thermometer is taped to the subject's finger who is then asked to 'will' the finger to get hot, with all the force that can be summoned, then the result is that in less than a minute the finger gets considerably <u>colder</u>! This is because strong use of the will invokes the basic primitive "fight-or-flight" brain response which causes physiological changes such as diversion of blood from the skin to the muscles ready for some violent action. To make the finger warmer it is necessary to use imagination not will. Imagine putting the hand in warm water or near the fire. A change of 2 degrees should easily be obtained at the first attempt and much more with practice. If the meter reads over 35.5°C, imagine the hand in ice cold water, to get a reduced reading.

Training thus, to increase hand temperature and decrease forehead temperature has been found to often result in control of migraine headaches. There are many simple medical uses of biofeedback.   E.g. electrodes are taped on each side of a muscle such as the frontalis (forehead) muscle, and the signal from it is made visible to <u>subjects</u> with severe facial tics or with insomnia; by seeing the image of his muscle signals on the screen, the person is able to change it (simply by imagining it to change) which alleviates these conditions considerably. Similarly tension headaches have been treated thus, because frontalis relaxation is generally accompanied by similar relaxation of the scalp and neck muscles (5). It is however very important that one should be sitting comfortably and resting the head so that no muscular neck strain should occur due to bad posture.

Biofeedback can apply to a signal from brainwaves (EEG), skin resistance (which indicates relaxation), muscular tension, heart beat, skin temperature etc., and whatever is thus fed back to the subject can be controlled by him. Once the knack is learnt, the biofeedback machine is no longer necessary and can be dispensed with: the <u>subject</u> is the controller - not the machine. The more times the alpha or theta state is experienced, the more inner benefit is gained. Eventually the ability is gained to enter these states without the biofeedback machine connected.

All sound-and-light machines (discussed in the next chapter) inherently allow biofeedback, due to an effect discovered by Maxwell Cade (see next chapter).

CHAPTER 7

SYNCHRONISING OF THE LEFT & RIGHT BRAIN
HEMISPHERE
BY SOUND & LIGHT

Ancient ways for entering higher State of Consciousness by Light and Sound:

The effects of light and sound are not a new discovery. Before recorded history, the mesmerising effect of flickering firelight and tribal drum beats were noted for creating trance-like states; these have now been replaced by the beat of pop music and disco flashing units!

Ptolemy, in 200 A.D., recorded that the flickering of sunlight through the spokes of a rotating wheel can cause fascinating visual patterns and euphoria. Nostradamus in the 13th century gained visual images by quickly passing his opened fingers between his eyes and sunlight... . The thing that is new is the remarkable application of advanced electronics to this phenomenon.

Reported benefits of light & sound machines

♦Relaxation & Creativity:

- produce relaxation & relieve stress
- produce visual imagery
- exploring the subconscious - easy entry to meditative states
- fast achievement of deep meditative states
- increase creativity & inventive ability by bringing out the **intuitions** which cause all kinds of vitally important creative work, ranging from Scientific & Engineering invention to the composing of great music and Art
- achieve hypnotic states
- relief from insomnia

♦Educational

- produce high speed learning, even of boring material! This is of special value for students!
- improve memory
- increase I.Q.!
- equalise the activity of both brain hemispheres, to bring out latent abilities

Brain Activity

The brain consists of two hemispheres:
The **right** hemisphere is artistic & **intuitive**.
The **left** hemisphere is logical & **deductive**.

Many people are normally active mainly in the left (problem solving) hemisphere and their right (intuitive, artistic) hemisphere lies fairly dormant. To achieve our maximum abilities we need to balance our brain hemispheres' activities. Light & sound machines are very effective in placing both hemispheres into highly desirable **balanced** states with increased awareness & creativity.

Sound

About 10 years ago I visited Robert Monroe (7) in the Blue Ridge Mountains in Virginia (USA). He runs an institute for investigating consciousness. His institute has developed a method of changing both frequency and phase of sound waves. Listening to a sound pulse which is repeated at, say, 10 times per second, should 'drive' the brain into the alpha frequency, but because the mind soon learns to reject a repetitive noise (e.g. a clock ticking at night is soon not perceived), this method does not work. Monroe sidestepped this ability of the brain by applying a tone of, say 100 Hz to one ear and 110 Hz to the other, so that the beat or difference frequency of 10 Hz is produced in the mind and is not rejectable by the brain. This has proved to be a powerful technique. The most effective frequencies are in the low hundreds of Hz (e.g. 250 and 240 Hz to produce 10 Hz).

This beat frequency is very effective in balancing the hemispheres and driving the brain and at the beat frequency. The subject can be taken and held into any of the stages of sleep, from alpha through theta into delta and REM sleep (i.e. dreaming sleep). Monroe has taken out a patent on this method. By this means he set up an "explorer group" for 'astral projection' (7-12, 34, 37-40) at will.

Incidentally, Monroe mentions that a focused but relaxed state of prayer or meditation can also produce synchronisation of the hemispheres. He believes that his method creates new neural pathways between the brain hemispheres.

Pre-recorded tapes are now available which produce such beat frequencies which can produce effects similar to light and sound machines in inducing the theta state etc. For further information on this effect of beat frequencies, see reference (31, 80).

More recently, The Monroe Institute has performed research into EEG mapping from brain areas (see back cover of book for a typical brain wave map after using a light and sound machine) and has made advances into binaural beat technology as described later in this chapter. Objective proof of the effect of binaural beats has been well established in many EEG studies, showing the brainwave state does change (131).

What are SOUND AND LIGHT MACHINES?

There are several models. Essential components are:
1) a small control unit, 2) goggles or eyeglass frames that position tiny lights in front of each eye, 3) stereo head-phones, 4) stereo-tape input socket for effortless super-learning, 5) instruction manual. The control unit is a sophisticated micro-computer that regulates the frequency & intensity of the rhythmic pulsing sounds & flickering lights. Most control units contain pre-programmed sessions with various combinations of sound & light frequencies designed to help you reach desired states. Some units allow the user to create his or her own programmes.

Driving the Brain's frequency with Light & Sound

A light & sound machine uses pulses of slowly falling frequency which lead the mind from its normal waking consciousness to deeper, more relaxed states in which intuitive regions are reached. This frequency following is called 'entrainment'. Everyone can benefit from one or more of the features listed above.

Light & sound machines can facilitate entry to various brainstates in a controlled way. If some *beta* (wakefulness) is maintained while passing through the *alpha* (relaxation) state to the *theta* (imagery) state, then sleep will not follow uncontrollably. The remarkable properties of the theta state can then be consciously explored (rather than merely dreamed).

In outline, light and sound machines start at the beta frequency and slowly lead the brain frequencies down to the lower alpha & theta states. Leading further down to lower frequencies induces delta (sleep) in just a few minutes if there is no simultaneous stimulation of beta (wakefulness). The effect of several hours of normal sleep can be gained in about 15 minutes by using a light & sound machine to hold the brain in the delta state. The benefits of induced relaxation are very great, ranging from tension & stress relief to removing jet-lag travel effects. All light and sound machines allow dual users, with the correct matching eyepieces.

Bio-feedback from an EEG unit can be added: if one can immediately perceive the effect of entering a particular mental state, this is found to greatly enhance the ability to re-enter that state at will. This feature is available on some of the machines. However, as mentioned in Chapter 6, a form of biofeedback is inherently available in all light and sound machines (see Fig. 4, page 59).

Three basic requirements for brainwave entrainment are:
(i) resonance: the brain must be capable of oscillating at the desired frequency;
(ii) power: the driving frequency signal must have sufficient strength (i.e. sound volume);
(iii) constancy (isochronicity): the driving frequency signal must have its peaks equally spaced and must have a true "off" in between pulses.

If someone is highly stressed, he/she will have strong beta brainwaves which will not entrain to (say) 10 Hz (alpha). Such an anxiety state may be due to diverse factors like too much coffee, anxiety about the experiment or about one's job etc., or wilfully not letting the strobe be 'in control'. It is essential to make the decision to let the strobe entrain (drive) the brain's frequency. It is advisable to listen to a relaxation tape before using a light & sound machine. Alternatively, the strobe could be set to start near the subject's beta frequency (say about 24 Hz) and then the entrainment will be very much more effective than just starting the strobe at the desired end frequency (10 Hz). If a strobe were set at 12 Hz, which is (say) half the actual brainwave frequency of the subject, it would actually reinforce the 24 Hz (being its first sub-harmonic)!

Binaural beats from an external sound source can only be detected if the sound is < 1000 Hz (cycles per second), because below 1000 Hz the wavelength of sound is greater than the diameter of the skull. Such external sounds (< 1000 Hz) can curve around the outside of the skull by diffraction and can thus be heard by both ears, but because of the distance between the two ears the sounds are out of phase (i.e. the peaks in the sound waveform arrive at slightly different times at the two ears). This is why sounds < 1000 Hz can be accurately located & is why most animal sounds are < 1000 Hz (with some specialised exceptions). A phase difference causes binaural beats (interference frequency): see Fig. 5 (page 59). However, if <u>earphones</u> are used to feed the two signals to each ear, there is no external physical sound wave interference as in Fig. 5, but the <u>brain</u> still detects a phase difference and the brain is thus forced to perceive an (apparent) beat frequency (the beats are not actually 'heard' but one thinks that they are being heard!).

Entrainment rule (i) above means that such a beat frequency must be < 30 Hz or it will not entrain the brainwaves. Subjects do not report 'hearing' binaural beats at above 30 Hz (129).

Each brain hemisphere has a sound centre which receives signals from each ear, causing two standing waves equal in amplitude & frequency, in each brain hemisphere, which entrain each hemisphere. There are more cross-connections however, than direct connections (i.e. the right ear has more connections to the left brain sound centre than to the right brain sound centre, and vice-versa). Thus, unusually, to specifically activate principally the right hemisphere (say) the volume of the hemi-sync signal to the left ear must be increased & that to the right ear be decreased.

The brain has vertical divisions as well as the horizontal division into hemispheres (this is explained in Chapter 10). Each vertical brain component resonates at a certain frequency at which it is conscious (130). The Monroe Institute has developed complex mixes of hemi-sync beat frequencies to activate these various brain areas in specific ways to achieve specific states of consciousness. Much valuable research has been done by the Monroe Institute; 'hemi-sync' is their registered trademark.

Their famous "Focus-10" state (mind awake, body asleep) entrains the cerebellum (controls body functions & muscles) to delta (sleep), and the cortex (seat of mind, consciousness) to theta (visual imagery, dream state). The cerebellum is first exposed to delta beats & the cortex later to theta. The subject becomes unaware of where his hands and feet etc. are, but does not lose consciousness (fall asleep). Such pre-recorded tapes are available (enquire from the publishers of this book). The user aims to eventually learn how to achieve various states of consciousness without the tapes.

Brainwave entrainment is not confined to the application of beat frequencies. It has been found that if a water bed is fed with a vibratory frequency, this will also entrain a subject's brainwaves to that frequency. Light & sound machines are also very effective in entrainment.

Results of Entrainment by Light & Sound

It is well known that with flashing lights or stroboscopes, it is possible to drive the brain's electrical   oscillations at the flashing light's frequency. Similarly, sound will drive the brain's oscillations. Infrasound, sound waves below the audible range, below about 20 Hz, is generated by some winds like the sirocco, and has very negative mental effects, well documented.   Earthquakes owe part of their terror to the infrasound which they generate, which disorients the mind by disrupting the normal beta frequency in it. Old single-decker buses can sometimes have roof oscillation at around 10 Hz (cycles per second), which is not exactly audible but is manifest as a buffeting sensation which blocks out normal thinking.

Infrasound weapons have been developed to disorient the thinking of an enemy.

A less objectionable use is in a disco where a strong sound beat drives the brain at a hypnotic frequency, in the theta/alpha range, an effect which is increased by the simultaneous use of synchronised flashing lights. A more objectionable use was the continuous round-the-clock powerful radio transmission known to amateur radio operators as "the woodpecker", which it sounds just like. These signals were the most powerful radio transmission in the world, of transmission frequency around 16 MHz, and they emanated from the USSR. Their repetition frequency of 10 Hz was in the centre of the alpha brainwave band. When the brain is oscillating at this frequency, thinking becomes impossible. The aerials of this transmitter were arranged so that these sinister oscillations could not be heard in the then Soviet Union, but could be heard everywhere else. This was a very unwelcome form of electromagnetic pollution.

In case you may think that radio waves do not affect us, it is known that certain radar frequencies are perceived, by everyone, as a hissing noise, apparently located above and behind the head. Depression due to mains 50 Hz frequency radio waves from power lines is discussed below. A few people can hear radio programmes in their head, without using a receiver. They thought they had become psychic, but actually this rare effect is due to a loose filling in a tooth, which acts both as detector and loudspeaker!

The light and sound machines or 'mind machines' now commercially available for driving (entraining) the brainwave frequency, combine both flashing light strobing and synchronised sound beats which are very effective in driving the brainwaves to desirable states. One currently available light and sound machine, the Alphapacer, also contains a synchronised electromagnetic transmitter which is believed to enhance its effect.

The complex patterns seen are in the mind of the perceiver (5). Light and sound strobes are very useful to use before or during meditation.

People living near mains power lines become irritable and sometimes depressed; this is because 50 cycles per second borders on the upper part of the beta brainwave band. A big beta output from the brain is synonymous with a stress situation. So irritability is not surprising, if the brain is driven at a beta frequency by proximity to mains power lines, or even, perhaps, by night- long proximity to bedside mains-powered radios and lamps with mains flexes (112, 117-122).

Anthropologists have found that shamans use drum frequencies in the theta range to enhance their claimed ability to enter states of visual imagery. Music is of course well-known for its consciousness altering powers; the brain-state of listeners is altered by the rhythms and frequencies used.

Gray Walter, the first modern researcher into flashing light reported, "The rhythmic series of flashes appear to be breaking down some of the physiologic barriers between different regions of the brain. This means the stimulus of flicker received by the visual projection area of the cortex was breaking bounds - its ripples were overflowing into other areas. Subjects reported lights like comets, ultra-unearthly colours, mental colours, not deep visual ones." These reports interested the novelist Burroughs, who investigated the effect and reported, "Subjects report dazzling lights of unearthly brilliance and colour. Elaborate geometric constructions of incredible intricacy build up from multidimensional mosaic into living fireballs like the mandalas of eastern mysticism or resolve momentarily into apparently individual images and powerfully dramatic scenes like brightly coloured dreams." Later researchers showed that the addition of synchronised sound beats greatly increased the effects (49).

Recently, an authority on anaesthesia, Cosgrove, commented that a light and sound machine is an excellent neuropathway exerciser, "the long term effects of regular use of the device on maintaining and improving cerebral performance thoughout life and possibly delaying for decades the deterioration of the brain traditionally associated with ageing is very exciting. We plan to test this hypothesis in brain-injured patients where the degree of recovery has been proven to be related to sensory and cerebral stimulus, with the results having implications for long-term use in healthy normal brains." Other researchers have reported large proportions of migraine sufferers have had their migraines stopped by flashing light stimulation, with brighter light being significantly more effective. AIDS sufferers have received benefit in the form of improved immune function by producing states of deep relaxation in which visualisation of healing is enhanced (Harris, Penwell Foundation, USA)(49).

Harrah-Conforth recently completed a study involving a control group who only received pink noise stimulation and a main group who received light and sound stimulation. He found that the latter group showed major alterations of their EEG patterns and brain hemispheric synchronisation. He reports comments like, "I lost all sense of my body", "I felt like I was flying", "I was deeply relaxed", "I felt like I was out of my body". He suggests that light and sound machines may cause simultaneous arousal of the sympathetic nervous system plus cerebral cortex and arousal of the parasympathetic system which is linked to "the timeless, 'oceanic' mode of the mystic experience." He concludes that these two states may be viewed as hyper-arousal (ecstasy) and hypo-arousal (samadhi)(49).

Recent research by Isaacs and Megabrain Inc shows that there is "very clear evidence of brainwave driving" by light and sound machines, with very strong correlation to the intensity of the lights used, both for red LEDs and incandescent bulbs. Dim lights have no brain driving effect (49).

Isaacs also found that during frequency-driving (entrainment) to lower frequencies, alpha is readily obtained but on driving lower the theta produced is often at a different frequency from the flashing light. He explains this as due to the brain becoming "used to" the repetitive stimulus and the reticular activating system (RAS, explained in Chapter 10) then steps in and blanks out the conscious perception of the lights. The result is that the brain then drops into the theta state. This effect may be observed during use of light & sound machines. The effect could be similar to that of the ganzfeld device (See Chapter 10) which obtains a blank-out effect by presenting a uniform featureless non-pulsing (steady) light which fills the entire field ("ganzfeld") of view (49).

Stress-related irrelevant jaw-muscle activity is a significant problem for some people, causing involuntary grinding of their back teeth while asleep. This effect is substantially reduced by the D.A.V.I.D. light & sound machine. Similarly dental research has shown that the muscular tension of holding one's mouth open (digastric muscles) against the jaw-closing (masseter) muscles, which often causes a stiff neck in dental patients, can be prevented by use of a light & sound machine at alpha frequency.

Chronic pain can be managed with light & sound machines (132)   Reduced medication, lower suicide ideation, decreased stress, better sleep and other beneficial effects are reported. The findings are discussed in terms of endorphin production (see Chapter 5) and relaxation response.

Super-learning can occur in the theta state, with no problem of attention wandering or boredom!   In this state, knowledge can be absorbed uncritically (whether interesting or boring) and at about 3 times the 'normal' rate. Self- made lesson tapes can be superimposed from your 'Walkman' onto the sound channel of a light & sound machine; an input jack is provided for the purpose.   Users of such systems include businessmen & women, scientists, engineers, artists, music composers (because of the intuitive & creative abilities enhancement), students, hospitals, athletes, insomnia sufferers, people under tension & stress, people interested in exploring meditative states, etc.

General Information on Entrainment:

Flashing lights & pulsing tones cause a brainwave resonance in the visual & auditory cortex, which in turn causes resonance in adjacent brain areas. These areas in turn then cause resonance in further areas. This process is called the frequency following response, or 'entrainment', causing the subject to drift into a meditative/hypnotic state accompanied by muscular relaxation.

The brain will follow pulsing lights, pulsing sounds, pulsing magnetic fields and, most strongly of all, pulsing electrical waves when applied directly. Light & sound entrainment by themselves tend not to persist after the light & sound pulses are turned off, but do produce a genuine effect on brainwaves while on, which can be shown on an electro-encephalograph (EEG). Binaural beats as the sound source is more effective, but the effect also dissipates quickly after the sound is turned off. Only with some practice in meditation methods, can this dissipation be avoided. But the dissipation effect is found to be much reduced if pulsed electrical waves are applied directly to the body (similar to electrical acupuncture). The most effective waveform is pulsed pink noise, as used in the Alphapacer III +. Adding the other synchronous stimulations available (magnetic, light & sound pulses) increased the entrainment effect. Even short times spent daily, or less often, in a theta state will be very beneficial.

Biofeedback by Light and Sound Machines:

All Light and sound machines inherently allow biofeedback due to the following effect discovered by Maxwell Cade:

If red or green colours are observed, this means that predominantly beta waves are being produced. If white or yellow, then mainly alpha is being generated; if blue, mauve and deep purple are seen, then mainly theta is being produced. This is tabulated opposite.

This biofeedback will greatly help in achieving brainwave control, i.e. in learning how to alter one's brain-state to and from any of the 3 major types (beta, alpha, theta).

Fig. 4

Biofeedback of brain-state:
Colours seen using Light and Sound machines and
corresponding brainwave states.

Colour field perceived	Brainwave State
red	beta
green	beta
white	alpha
yellow	alpha
blue	theta
mauve	theta
deep purple	theta

(a)

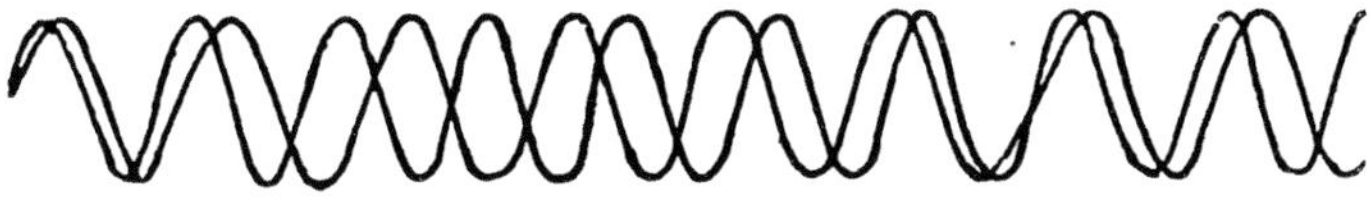

(b)

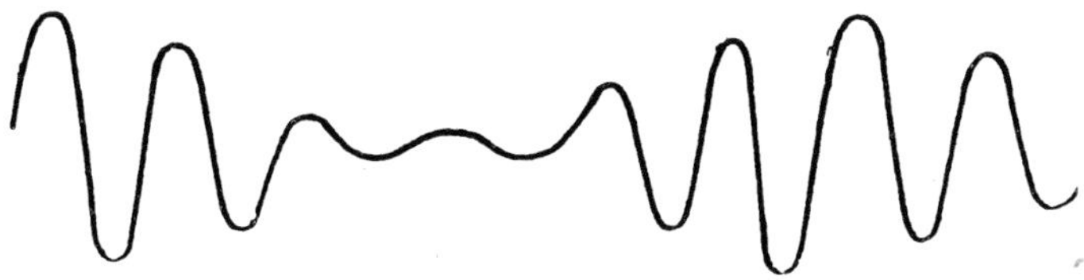

Fig. 5 (a) two co-existing waves of different wave lengths.
(b) resultant wave produced by addition of these waves.

Relaxation & Meditation Enhancement:

Experienced meditators produce a preponderance of alpha brainwaves and those with many years practice produce theta also (e.g. Zen & yoga methods). It normally takes years to achieve these states. Even such methods as biofeedback with an EEG display takes quite a while to master (but the effort is well worth while). The Alphapacer III+ and similar mind machines will help one to experience these relaxed and meditation-like states rapidly. It should be noted however, that single frequency electronically induced states will be similar, but not identical, to naturally produced meditation states because the latter do not consist of one brainwave frequency alone. Most mind machines induce one frequency, but there are some which induce two (and thence, by interference or beat, three). Fig. 2 shows EEG traces of correct meditation states with 3 frequencies: some beta, alpha and theta. Of course, just successfully inducing one is a big step forward from none at all!

Higher range alpha is useful for light relaxation and for fast learning. Lower alpha frequencies are ideal to induce deep relaxation & meditation. As the frequencies are lowered into the theta range many people experience imagery and an awareness of material from the subconscious. Deeper meditation experiences occur in this lower range. Access to personal creativity can also be enhanced by the induction of alpha and theta brainwave states. Greater integration of one's conscious and unconscious minds may also result from this conscious opening to deeper brainwave states; integration of awareness from left and right brain hemispheres is produced by the equalising effect of light and sound machines on the brainwave amplitudes from each hemisphere. This is an important feature for creativity.

Low sound frequencies echoing from monastery walls alters consciousness and causes brain biochemical effects. This eventually produces a state of enlightenment. Hence the chanting of monks, particularly Tibetan chants at very low frequency. The latter are available, for example, in 'Dorge Ling' by D. Parsons (available from CMC Ltd). This take many years and light & sound machines, beat frequency tapes and flotation tanks greatly accelerate the process. Instead of you meditating, they 'meditate' you!

Technical Comments:

Superbright red light-emitting diodes (LEDs) have a very fast switch-on brightness rise, which causes simultaneous firing of numerous retinal neurons. Some special white filament lamps are available with very fast rise times of 7 milliseconds (which is in fact faster than the eye receptors can respond).

White light flashes are more effective in reducing anxiety than red. There are divergent opinions on whether white or red light is more effective for entrainment. Red light is probably more effective than xenon strobe white light but this does not apply to fast rise incandescent lamps (which have a controllable 'on' time, unlike xenon strobes).

Red light is much more effective than other single colours for brainwave entrainment; this does not apply to special fast-rise white incandescent bulbs which are as effective as red LEDs.

An important feature is isochronicity of sound pulses, i.e. the pulses should appear at precisely the same time intervals (no 'jitter') and also the ratio of 'on' intensity to 'off' intensity should be at least 200 to 1 to produce brainwave entrainment.

Eyelids are very good diffusing screens, blurring point LEDs to a ganzfeld of wide uniform featureless lighting; e.g. if the sun is faced, with closed eyelids, a uniform ganzfeld is seen.

Stimulation of retinal cones of one type is reduced if others of a different colour sensitivity are also stimulated, but this effect may not be significant in <u>comparison with other important factors.</u>

A few light & sound machines allow different frequencies to be presented to each eye & ear, giving intermodulation with extraordinary psychedelic imagery. E.g. theta in one eye and beta in the other, giving "mind awake, body asleep" and other special states. The beat frequency produced generates enhanced states (e.g. from 15 Hz RHS & 10 Hz LHS, 5 Hz is obtained, which is, fortuitously, the theta frequency).

Precaution: It is sensible to allow half an hour after using light and sound machines and other mind enhancing units and tapes before operating machinery or driving a car.

CHAPTER 8

ELECTRO-ENCEPHALOGRAPH (EEG) UNITS

An EEG is an electronic detector which records and amplifies the signals emitted by our brain. Several electrodes are used. One is affixed to the forehead, two to the ear lobes and two halfway between the ears and the back of the head.

Grey Walter, in 1954, developed an EEG with 22 visual output channels. About 10 years ago, Maxwell Cade and Geoffrey Blundell produced a similar device which they called the 'Mind Mirror' (5). The output is displayed on a screen which one can be viewed thus allowing biofeedback (by imagining a change in the output which makes it actually occur and change on the screen). This has 12 channels (frequencies) for each hemisphere of the brain, i.e. 24 channels in all. Another version is now available. Although the results are very impressive, a disadvantage of EEGs is the need to hold electrodes onto the head to pick up the microvolt size signals there. This can be overcome by using dry self-adhesive electrodes behind the ears where there is a patch of bare skin, with a third electrode on the forehead. But then the electrical activity is that of the whole hemispheres rather than that from the occipital regions only, which latter is obtained if 5 electrodes are used [one (earth) on the forehead, two at the ears and two more about halfway between ears and back of head]. But any electrode in a region of hair cannot be a self-adhesive type and a wet gel pad is needed. Fig. 2 shows the type of display produced by the Mind Mirror (5).

Many years ago I attended one of Maxwell Cade's workshops where everyone had a chance to use a Mind Mirror EEG. The results of EEG biofeedback are impressive (5). EEG users should refer to reference (5), which also contains exercises for relaxation and visual imagery.

Some gifted people can produce advanced patterns on the mind mirror immediately - e.g. Sir George Trevelyan, founder of the Wrekin Trust, could immediately produce a big circle.

Note that "just alpha" is not really a meditational or inner awareness state because the latter requires simultaneous sidebands of theta and beta. Display of all these bands together (Fig. 2) shows the value of the Mind Mirror - to observe one's own pattern and get it into the proper multiband states by this biofeedback process.

Practical EEG Biofeedback Results

A typical aim is to generate an alpha output with the eyes open. This requires us to observe-without-looking (stare into space), i.e. disinterestedly. It is possible to learn how to hold this state and even answer simple questions without losing it. But the first step is to produce alpha with the eyes closed, of course.

The next step is the "theta reverie", in which a theta output is produced and very clear visual images appear spontaneously without us being aware of their origin or creation. This state corresponds to descriptions by geniuses of the past who wrote descriptions of their state of consciousness while at their most creative.

Alpha production can easily be learned with open eyes but initially theta is usually possible only with closed eyes. Theta images are so tenuous that open eyes drive them away.

Green and Walters in Kansas (4) have worked in this area. They made tests on a trained yogi, Swami Rama, from Rishikesh. He produced alpha simply by "thinking of an empty blue sky" and theta by "stilling the conscious mind and bringing forward the unconscious". He said **pure** alpha is literally nothing, but **pure** theta is a "very noisy" state in which things he should have done and associated images rushed up and shouted at him etc. In a **pure** theta state he was clearly a prey to suppressed worries in spite of his training. This is similar to experiences reported with psychedelic drugs, a state of visual imagery but with suppressed problems magnified and reflected back at one. The psychedelic drug state appears similar to the theta state that can be developed by EEG biofeedback. EEG training or the easier and cheaper light and sound machines and hemisphere synchronisation tapes offer an acceptable way to replace the drugs problem and this could be of immense importance. Swami Rama generally avoided a (pure) theta state. He demonstrated delta also, after 5 minutes lying down with his eyes closed. He repeated back some words which had been spoken in the room during his apparent sleep. He said that 15 minutes of this 'yogic sleep' as he called it is equivalent to an hour's normal sleep. He said in the delta state both his brain and mind were asleep, he told the mind to be quiet, not to respond to anything but to record everything, and to remain tranquil until activated. The Mind's Eye Courier light and sound machine has a 'jet lag' programme which makes use of the foregoing effect, but without needing years of yogic training.

Swami Rama could diagnose illness like Edgar Cayce except he was totally conscious but indrawn briefly while picking up the information. He said he wants to give a training programme for medical doctors. I have already mentioned that Maxwell Cade discovered psychic healing ability in people by looking for delta wave production.

When Swami Rama produced alpha he did not have to cease beta production. When producing theta, he was able (and preferred) to simultaneously produce both alpha and beta, each for about 50% of the time. Alpha is a conscious state and it may be necessary to keep it going when theta is produced, in order to be aware of and have some control of the imagery of the theta state. This idea is supported by research by Green et al who trained some subjects in Swami Rama's breathing method: this consists of deep and slow rhythmic breathing at a constant rate both in and out with no pauses at the top and bottom of the breathing cycle. After 4 or 5 months, with at least 10 days per month doing this exercise, their breathing rate could be slowed down to one or two per minute for 10 minutes. This agrees with observations by Wallace (5) that a considerable drop in metabolism accompanies the practice of 'transcendental meditation' (the system publicised by Maharishi Mahesh Yogi). Swami Rama took some EEG machines back to India and said they would speed up the training of yogis.

Swami Rama and others say that self-healing can be performed in a state of deep reverie. The Silva method is similar (18). Images for giving the body instructions are used while in the theta state. Theta brain wave training narrows the gap between the conscious and unconscious states. In the theta state the body can be programmed at will and the instructions will be carried out. Emotional states can be objectively examined, accepted or rejected or totally replaced by others, and problems which are insoluble in the normal states of consciousness can be solved. ESP abilities in the theta state have been developed by EEG biofeedback.

It may be helpful to link the names of states of consciousness to brain waves: concentration = beta, meditation = alpha, contemplation = theta, satori = delta(?). It is not quite so simple; theta must be accompanied by some alpha and beta or consciousness is lost and sleep occurs.

Left-right hemisphere symmetry of brainwaves is long-term-improved by meditation and also, as Maxwell Cade found, by looking at a stroboscope. This symmetry adds your latent, intuitive and artistic abilities to your analytical and logical abilities, if you are an analytical type, or vice-versa if you are an artistic type. It has the same sort of effect as the alternophone or synchrophone of Lefebeure (24). It integrates your personality. The stroboscope has to emit orange-red flashes however, to be effective. This may induce abstract patterns or visual imagery as it DRIVES the brain at the theta frequency. It is better to start at the beta frequency and slowly drive the brain down to the theta state, but if anyone has a tendency to epilepsy it is necessary to avoid frequencies above about 16 Hz which could induce an epileptic condition in anyone who has epilepsy. In fact anyone with any type of seizure condition must take medical advice before using stroboscopic devices.

Wallace proposed that meditation (alpha) should be considered as a "fourth state of consciousness" and Goleman (5) proposed a fifth state in which the fourth state is infused into daily life. Alpha persists after the end of a Zen meditation practice. Maxwell Cade has held hundreds of seminars for EEG training. After about **4 hours** of training with the Mind Mirror the following results were noted for a large number of subjects (5):

1. All subjects, without exception, and usually at the first EEG training session, show a post-meditation phase with continuous alpha persisting about 10 minutes with open eyes (if the gaze is unfocused).
2. Alpha appears in two quite different states: One is pure alpha with only a few percent of other frequencies. This state is mindless, relaxed and neither thinking nor imagining. The other is high strength alpha with two continuous side bands (about 30 to 60% of the alpha amplitude) of steady frequency. One side band is beta at 16 to 18 Hz (waves per second) and the other is theta at 4 to 6Hz. This special alpha state is always symmetrical in both hemispheres of the brain. Subjects can open their eyes, hold conversations, and walk around. They can do mental arithmetic and experience self- induced emotional states, without losing the state. 'Testing' the state causes it to stop after about 10 minutes but it can always be restored by the subject adopting a passive attitude for a few minutes. Maxwell Cade believes this state is Goleman's "fifth state of consciousness".

If you want to read accounts of this "fifth state", see references (16,17 & 21). Paramhansa describes the transition from fourth to fifth state, called savikalpa samadhi and nirvikalpa samadhi, respectively. In the fourth state, a temporary realisation of oneness with Spirit is obtained but this 'cosmic consciousness' can't be held except in the immobile trance state. By continuous meditation the higher fifth state (nirvikalpa samadhi) is reached in which one can move freely in the world and perform one's duties without any loss of 'God-perception'. This transition can occur rapidly or take years, depending on the state of the nervous system of the individual. One attribute of the fifth state (22) is that pure awareness infuses the waking state and also the dreaming and sleep states. One can witness oneself entering the sleeping and dreaming processes, just as one can witness thought in meditation. This aspect of mind is called "The witness" by Gurdjieff (19).

Sleep & deep meditation are described as dissociative states by Atwater (131) and are accompanied by alpha suppression. "Resting state alpha" is alpha brainwaves confined to the back of the head. In a dissociative state, this alpha is suppressed which frees he mind from normal belief systems and opens the doors of perception to non-physical energies (131).

"Transcendence" is a further stage beyond dissociation, where one is beyond the limits of the ego and unconscious mind and into universal awareness. Experience of this state can alter the nature of the subject's reality (131). EEG maps show high amplitude delta and theta.

Cade & Coxhead (5) give an alternative description, described above, in terms of a "fourth state" (probably similar to the "dissociative state" of Atwater (131) and a "fifth state" (probably Atwater's "transcendence").

Procedures

Maxwell Cade found experimentally that obtaining the fifth state of consciousness is aided by special excercises to develop detachment. Subjects who can already produce continuous alpha or theta, to order, were trained to maintain these rhythms while visually scanning the surroundings, solving successively more difficult arithmetical problems, experiencing self-induced sensations of no-emotion, anger, hate, grief, love, joy and reverence, and finally walking about, and conversing with other people (while still maintaining the EEG pattern).

It must be emphasised that the brainwave state to aim at is not just pure alpha or theta, but is alpha ACCOMPANIED by unvarying side-bands in the theta and beta regions. The former states are, however, essential stepping stones to the latter fifth level. Before starting the exercises it is essential to go mentally up or down the body, relaxing all the muscles one by one.

Then the next step (using the Mind Mirror EEG, in this example) is to produce continuous alpha and theta by, for example, passive concentration on breathing. Breathing is the only body function that can be entirely automatic, as in sleeping, or entirely under mind control. It is used in many meditation systems just because it is a pivot between voluntary and involuntary control. The breathing exercises of meditation in which the breath can be imagined like a swinging door, have a hypnotic effect; one breathes at a frequency in the delta range.

Then incremental stressing can be used to infuse the alpha or theta with one's normal activity (5):

1) (a) Open eyes; look slowly and disinterestedly around the room without focusing on anything. If the alpha signal

disappears, rest and allow it to return. Do not restart these stressing exercises until the signal has remained steady for at least 30 seconds.

(b) Focus eyes sharply on various objects.

(c) Make eye contact with other people.

2) Solve mentally some simple arithmetic problems.

3) For 2 minutes each, feel each of these 7 emotions (= 1 cycle); then repeat the cycle:

(a) no emotion, just calmness; (b) anger; (c) hate; (d) grief; (e) love; (f) joy; (g) reverence.

4) Pick up your EEG machine (or as appropriate) and walk about talking to people. Stop and rest with closed eyes if you lose the signal.

Experience at these levels leads to permanent changes. With practice you can also recognise what brainwave state you are in, **without being connected to an EEG!** (The ultimate in biofeedback).

Most people do not have symmetrical left and right brainwaves patterns but only a few hours of mediation leads to symmetry - the balancing of the logical (left) and the intuitive (right).

Green et al describe a theta training project with a group of volunteers (4). To prevent them from drifting off to sleep (i.e. losing all of their beta), they used a type of alarm clock which would ring unless a bar on top was pressed which advanced the alarm setting by 7 minutes. Portable EEG's were lent to the volunteers who practised about an hour each weekday recording observations in a notebook. They were asked to increase the amount of theta produced and to report the visual

imagery. The imagery was classified into 7 groups:
mental events, physical events, symbolic content, personal content, transpersonal content, extrapersonal content.

Most subjects could easily increase alpha and increase theta with more difficulty. There was a big increase in the imagery. Many students reported integration of their personalities and increased vitality occurring with alpha- theta training. Memory and concentration also improved. Some reported an increased awareness of nature - colours, wind, trees, sky. Archetypal images were reported by many, such as:
travel through tunnels, up and down stairs, images of eyes, images of a wise man or of a book of knowledge.

There was increased awareness and recall of dreams and of forgotten events of childhood. These were not a memory but a **re-living** of the events, complete with sounds and smells and with great clarity.

ESP observations of events were also reported, including distant vision (4).

CHAPTER 9

PATHWORKING

Some background to this is given in Chapter 4, in the section on visual imagery.

Entries to the so-called astral level depend on visual imagery, developed by various methods. One method is hypnosis; in hypnosis visual images are easy to develop. Another way is through the Tarot, or other pathworking doorways (11,23,26). One has to create a picture of the doorway as a visual image and then imagine one's-self moving into it, to reach the astral level.

The series of books by Ashcroft-Nowicki (23) is highly recommended, along with reference (11). The method is to perform relaxation and breathing exercises. These can be very greatly enhanced by entering a theta state using a light and sound machine, a CES unit (see Chapter 11), or beat frequency type of tape, or a flotation tank (Chapter 10), before going on to the next stage. Light and sound machines have an input socket for tape recorder input and this can be used with a pre-recorded tape of the pathworking text given by Ashcroft-Nowicki, which involves imagining an old wooden door with massive iron hinges, seeing every detail in the mind's eye. Through the door is a wild moorland on one side and on the other side a set of cliffs washed by a grey, wind-tossed sea. You next lock the door, placing the key in your pocket and a detailed pathworking journey follows (23), using ancient archetypal paths defined (for example) by traditional tarot cards' scenes (Fig. 6). Tarot card no XXI is an 'astral doorway', the path between Malkuth (Earth) and Yesod (astral or dreamworld) in Kabbalistic terms (103). After this, returning through the door and locking it behind you, it is important to ensure that you are fully back in your own space and time. Feel the chair and floor beneath you, get up and walk around and have something to eat and drink. Eating and drinking is the quickest and safest way to close down the doorways to the imagination after an inner exploration.

Surprising revelations from your deep subconscious may be obtained by this method, even if you are not familiar with the tarot.

Paraliminal tapes are a recent invention in which one ear hears one story and the other another, but these have not yet been developed for pathworking.

Another entry to the astral level is by interrupting a dream while asleep. During dreaming the emotional disturbance caused by the dream produces an increase in breathing rate. A temperature sensor called a thermistor can easily be attached to the nostril with adhesive tape and it changes its resistance with temperature; one's outbreath is warmer than the inbreath. The thermistor's resistance changes are measured and when these changes exceed a preset frequency (due to faster breathing) another circuit delivers a very small electric shock to a wrist band and the dreamer is thereby alerted IN the dream to the fact that he IS dreaming and he can then become self-conscious in the dream. An alternative to a nasal thermistor is a ribbon around the chest with an (inexpensive) flat strain gauge on it, whose resistance changes with each chest expansion (breath).

Dreams occupy about 20% of total sleep time, about 90 minutes each night. During dreaming, rapid eye motion (REM) occurs. A recently available unit ("Dreamlight") uses the direct method of sensing eye motion electronically and immediately sending a train of flashes to a tiny light (LED) fixed in a simple mask (like the ones issued on air flights to exclude light, for those who wish to sleep). The person wearing this mask will then see, in the dream, a brightening-up of the scene or perhaps flashing jewels appear (or some other event) which will trigger off the memory of wearing the mask before sleeping with the intention of becoming aware in the dream. Then immediately, the dream becomes vivid or lucid and the dreamer becomes aware and can control instead of merely being a bystander. The effect is remarkable and the experience is highly recommended. The benefits obtainable from awareness during dreams were outlined in Chapter 1. Some useful references are (7-11 & 32- 40). Reference 34 has been verified by an acquaintance of the author to produce results.

CHAPTER 10

SENSORY DEPRIVATION - FLOTATION TANKS

Flotation tanks

This section tells of the remarkable effects obtained from a very simple procedure: merely floating on 10 inch deep pool of water in a dark enclosed chamber less than 8 feet by 4 feet in size. Of all the methods described in this book, this and CES (cranial electrical stimulation) are the most universal in their effect.

Sensory Deprivation:

At first, the mind will do anything to prevent the removal of the sensory input to which it has got used. Research has been done on the effect of sensory deprivation on volunteers in a black room (25). People stay in a totally black room in total silence. After an initial long period of sleep their brainwaves drop to lower frequencies spontaneously. They see bright visions. A faster method is to float in a bath of very dense solution of Epsom salt in water controlled at normal skin temperature, in the dark and silence. This removes all the senses (touch, sound and vision) and one has no sensation of even having a body because its boundary (the skin) cannot be sensed. Remarkable results have been reported (6,2,41). This is discussed below.

The flotation tank has water only 10 inches deep but it contains 800 pounds weight of Epsom salts to give extreme buoyancy. An air pump provides ventilation. The optimum water temperature of 93.5°F is maintained by a thermostat. At this temperature it is impossible to feel the water (by its temperature) and so you cannot distinguish where your skin ends and the water begins! Also, in a fluid you have no sensation of any pressure (unlike lying on a bed). Such floating completely removes the sense of touch. It is comparatively easy to remove the other senses (vision - just keep out light; sound - just keep out noises; taste - just don't eat!; smell - just don't have any scented materials around). Clearly, of the 5 senses, touch is the most difficult to avoid. It requires a flotation tank.

Flotation feels like being weightless in black silent space and it is difficult to know if you are on your back or front or vertical. But there is no vertigo or discomfort nor any kind of claustrophobic sensation. As each part of one's body becomes relaxed, it seems to vanish from awareness until there is nothing left but consciousness. It is an almost indescribable experience, unlike anything else whatever. Soon after this, visualised events brightly appear, often scenes from childhood.

On emerging from an hour in the tank, the world seems to have changed in your absence! Things are seen anew - the world is fresh, illuminated, glowing bright, luminous, intensified. William Blake described such an awareness as "cleansing the doors of perception"; see Aldous Huxley's book of this title (1). Tests on subjects of sensory deprivation experiments show beneficial results such as increased visual acuity, tactile sense, auditory sensitivity and taste sensitivity, lasting up to 2 weeks (41). Improved learning, memory, IQ scores, perceptual motor tasks, enhanced visual concentration and increased short term visual storage also resulted.

Some physiologists estimate about 85% of our brain's activity is spent in dealing with and counteracting gravity. The effect of gravity is annulled in flotation and this releases a large proportion of brain activity. This quasi- release from gravity also allows blood circulation more freely, reaching parts not well-supplied due to cardiovascular constriction (due to smoking, cholesterol clogging, tension, etc.) and this reduces the effort needed by the heart. The blood pressure falls beneficially and the pulse rate slows. Relief of gravity-caused pressure on joints etc. will alleviate temporarily chronic pain due to arthritis, sprains etc.

Lilly & Shurley were the pioneers of flotation (6) and laid the foundations, but following Ptolemy's 1800 year-old account of the mental effects of a stroboscope (a spinning spoked wheel between closed eye and sun), one is tempted to speculate on the use of the deep sarcophagus in the Great Pyramid which can still be seen there, and in which one can lie (100, 111). There is nothing new under the sun...(42)!

The granite coffer in the Great Pyramid is over 6 ft 6 inches long and over 2 ft wide (internal measurements) and is too wide to go through the door. Clearly it would not have been removed by those who put it there, so the inference must be that they did not want 'those who came after' to remove it either. One may then speculate that they 'built it in' to be an 'indelible message' for those who came after. As a speculation, could the message be a recommendation to use a flotation tank to gain very easily the enormous benefits of deep meditative states? To speculate further, the Coptic Christians in Egypt are the lineal descendants of the Pharaonic or Osirian religion of ancient Egypt: Isis (or Asset), the mother of Horus, was replaced by Mary. Coptic churches contain large fonts. Churches across the world contain fonts; are these a 'folk-memory' that a religious building should contain a flotation tank? It is very likely that flotation tanks were used anciently as part of initiation procedures, but were kept secret and have since been forgotten. The Egyptian Mysteries were transmitted onwards to become the Greek Mysteries and were later passed on to Rome before almost disappearing in the Dark Ages.

Lilly (6) reports that he could control various states of consciousness while floating, such as waking dreams (vivid daydreams); events could occur with such brightness that they seemed real and could possibly be mistaken for events in the outside physical world. Truly an 'astral doorway' (see references 34, 37-40, 12, 7-11).

Meditation conventionally takes many years to achieve. To 'achieve' means, in measurable terms, the ability to go into a state in which the EEG trace is symmetrically bilateral and includes a small beta peak accompanied by larger alpha and theta peaks; see Fig. 2. But in a flotation tank these years of preparation (which overcome the external stimuli of touch and the other senses) are completely removed! It is 'instant mysticism'. People can go almost immediately to deep levels of meditation and contemplation (41, 72).

Psychological problems have also been rapidly solved in the tank: an acutely shy person became able to perform confident public speaking, to his amazement (41). Depression is linked to raised levels of pituitary & adrenal activity; floating is associated with decreases in these two activities. Hence it relieves depression.

Pain is substantially relieved by flotation and rates of recuperation increased. This includes cases of psychological damage as well as physical. Lawyers report greatly enhanced ability to marshal facts for cases during flotation, resulting in impressive results; this clearly can apply to any kind of job requiring mental organisation (41). In some cases even non-religious people have described flotation experiences as 'religious experiences'; it is clear that something very unusual indeed is occurring in the tank.

Green (4) points out that to produce theta consciously, it is necessary to have a quiet body, emotions and thoughts, simultaneously. It takes Zen monks some 20 years, but the flotation tank does it all for you in minutes! Studies have shown that after only 1 hour the theta level is significantly raised (without sleep intervening) (41). The tank is ideal for maintaining wakefulness while in theta (74). This is a very important remark. The tank is thus ideal for promoting creativity, as an example for the outer world; or for deep meditation, as an example for those interested in the inner world.

Maxwell Cade (5) discovered from studies of over 4000 people that unusual abilities like self-control of pain, healing, telepathy etc. are associated with changes in EEG pattern to a bilaterally symmetrical form (5). Other workers (and Maxwell Cade) (76-

78) found the same thing for those in deep meditation. The same happens during floating; the tank does not block left brain activity but makes it a partner with the right brain, whose activity floating brings forward (41).

Before trying floating, many people think it must be boring. In fact the opposite of boredom occurs. One floater said that every time she floated she felt like an explorer or adventurer and was proud of herself (41): consciousness - the ultimate frontier.

Some suggest the tank experience has obvious parallels with a return to the womb. Babies have theta brainwaves. Tanks cause increased endorphin levels (79); for comparison pregnant women have up to 8 times the usual blood endorphin level. Endorphins, like heroin & morphine, relieve pain & create euphoria.

An alternative to the "return to the womb" parallel may be replaced by a return to the paleontological environment of our distant ancestors, living in a warm sea (41).

Relaxation in the Tank

A common experience on entering the tank is to try hard to relax and not succeeding; but then, on just giving up trying, relaxation comes immediately! Relaxation comes without any effort being needed, very unlike in the world outside. Any efforts in the tank will cause hindrance. Biofeedback workers know this as the 'Law of Reversed Effort': whatever you "try" to do, the opposite result will be obtained. See the example given under BIOFEEDBACK (Chapter 6) - making one's finger hotter/colder. Like users of biofeedback machines, floaters soon learn the knack of 'letting go'. This knack becomes a 'body memory' and a familiar deep relaxation occurs in minutes after entering the tank (41). This state, once entered, is then ideal for beginning various techniques, such as: self-hypnosis, visualisation, healing, meditation, etc. and these work much more strongly in the tank. But the best advice is to set no such goals for the first few floats (41).

Deepening relaxation in the tank: Imagery

While avoiding the pitfall of over-trying to relax, just mentioned, focusing the mind on breathing helps relaxation. Relax the abdominal stomach area muscles. Try concentrating on the coolness at the tip of the nose on inhaling, and then the warmth there as you exhale. Try counting these from 1 to 10, repeatedly. Do not resist random thoughts but allow them to dissipate away.

Try concentrating your being in the centre of your forehead on a count of 1 breath. On breath 2, concentrate your being in your throat; 3 - right shoulder; 4 etc. - right elbow, wrist, each finger and back up arm to throat; similarly left arm; chest; abdomen; pelvis; right leg - toes - back up to pelvis; left leg; return up abdomen, to forehead. Each part will probably become warm and glowing as tension is released. Deep relaxation is achieved (41, 4).

Especially if you are a 'non-visualiser' type of person, practice visualising things while in the tank - e.g. a daffodil. You will find this remarkable & a profitable acquisition with many varied applications.

The above nose-breathing exercise can be combined with a visualisation to increase its effectiveness:

Visual imagery in the tank can be facilitated as follows (41): As you breathe in, visualise a pure white light entering your nostrils and going into your lungs & abdomen, thence radiating out to all parts of the body. On breathing out, imagine the reverse of this process. Exclude all thoughts from your mind except breathing.

On the in-breath, imagine the life-giving power of the oxygen and on breathing out imagine that as dark blue or grey, containing toxins, fatigue etc. which are being expelled. With this process, your body will slowly increase in brightness with time until the tank is filled with bright light.

A variant is to focus on a particular area of he body and visualise that as warmly glowing. This could be, for example, one of the chakras (113).

A further exercise in control of imagery is to imagine, for example, a blackboard and to 'see' on it various coloured shapes, such as a sphere, cube, pyramid, etc. Try a red triangle against a blue 'blackboard'. This is ideal for the so-called 'astral doorways' (11), which have well-defined shapes and colours, and as preparation for the Tarot astral doorway (Fig. 6).

You can also 'see' familiar cartoon figures from TV and imagine them dancing about.

An advanced visualisation is to imagine yourself getting smaller and smaller (like Alice in wonderland). Such visualisations have been described centuries ago by Patanjali (114), who indicates that a trained observer may be able to observe atoms. A century ago, trained meditators reported using this (claimed) ability and drew string-like pictures of what may be recognised today as strings of quarks. The author has discussed this extensively elsewhere (115). If such an ability could be

Fig. 6

Tarot Trump Card No. XXI
An "Astral Doorway"

From A.E. Waite Tarot deck.

developed, it would have profound scientific consequences. Similar visualisations stopping at the cellular level are the basis for the healing described below and in Chapter 4. Visualise entering your body & visiting various organs.

Further revealing visualisations are (41):

(1) Visualise someone well-known to you, face, skin texture, hair colour, eyes; see effect of a smile, of him/her moving, speaking (hear his/her voice) - note what is being said: probably important.

(ii) Visualise your own face; smile; notice all details. Anything you don't like? Visualise in some activity - like climbing. Let the image speak to you - what do you hear?

(iii) Visualise yourself in a scene from childhood.

The results of such visualisations will often surprise you and will reveal directly what is hidden in your mind.

Self-Hypnosis in the tank

Under self-hypnosis in the tank, Hutchison describes a successful self- diagnosis which proved correct (41 page 138). The tank is ideal for self- hypnosis, which requires deep relaxation and focused attention. People highly resistant to hypnosis and self-hypnosis can be hypnotised in the tank (135,136).

Children are right-hemisphere active, and if admonished by a parent saying "You're no good" etc., then this effectively powerfully negatively programmes the child and he/she needs to be deprogrammed later in life to remove the hidden blockage caused. This can be done under hypnosis or self-hypnosis. For self-hypnosis, try the standard method of counting backwards, but in the tank you will not need to count from 100 to 1 (conventional) but only from 10 to 1 due to the tank-conferred relaxation effect. Consult the many books on self-hypnosis for further details of procedure. Use the present tense in all hypnotic suggestions; try to image beneficial suggestions as being already true and make them as positive not negative ones (i.e. avoid using the word "not" in a suggestion) (41). Link them with an image where possible, for added power.

Suggestions are more effective if accompanied by stately, flowing melodious & light gentle background music.

For medically permissible pain relief, e.g. arthritis, imagine a bright light focused on the area, while in the tank (41). Floating has surprising & durable analgesic effects, due to endorphin release.

Superlearning

Many studies have conclusively demonstrated (41) that in a state of deep relaxation & focused attention, a state of hyper-suggestibility is reached where very fast learning of large amounts of information is possible. The tank is ideal for producing this state, due to the RAS 'turning up the volume' and to unusual access to the right-brain (41,). Light & sound machines can also perform this function, by placing the brain in the theta state.

In a survey (41) with a control group and a float tank group, taped chemistry lessons were heard, containing: (a) basic information, (b) application, (c) problem solving. Results showed floaters were better than the control group for (a), much better for (b) and very much better for (c). EEG traces showed greater theta waves for the floaters and this was shown to be related to the depth of understanding involved. It was also found that visualisation helps learning (41).

Lozanov (83) has invented a (non-tank) superlearning system in which a deeply relaxed state is invoked and while rhythmically breathing, the students listen to lessons spoken against slow background music (82).   The book, reference (82) is recommended as applicable to tank learning also. The deeper the state of relaxation, the more the student can learn.

Flotation tanks are available from CMC Ltd, 25 Lexham Garden, London W8 5JJ.

There is a Flotation Tank Association at 3A Elms Crescent, London SW4 8QE, & an associated one in the USA whose address is given in reference (41).

The relation of human brain evolution to Flotation:

The human brain evolved in 3 stages:

(1) the brain stem, from the reptilian period, (2) the limbic system (mammalian) and the cerebellum added to the stem, (3) the higher cortex. The last two of these are divided into left and right hemispheres. For more details, see reference (44).

A psychologist (70, 71) has remarked that the brain is hindered by a 'design error' - not enough communication between the higher cortex and the two older levels of the brain. This is a quite separate effect from the left/right hemispheres of the cortex; this lateral split is bridged by the corpus callosum and although industrial culture has caused left brain dominance, this can be corrected (there are ways to integrate & synchronise the left and right brains, as explained in this book). But the vertical division has few and slow connections.

In the (primitive) brain stem from the reptilian period, there is the 'reticular activating system' (**RAS**). This sets the arousal or awareness level. In the (advanced) cortex, all our advanced mental functioning occurs but the RAS is essential to keep the cortex awake. Consciousness is impossible if the RAS is destroyed.

Input from the senses to the cortex are passed to the RAS. If these signals are too intense, the RAS 'turns down' the brain's level of awareness (arousal state); if this fails, anxiety states occur. Conversely, if inputs from the senses are very low, as in sensory deprivation, then the RAS turns up the awareness of the cortex. This is the principle of the ganzfeld effect and of flotation tanks.

A ganzfeld device is an optical system which presents a uniform featureless light field to the eyes. As the RAS turns up the gain, visions may present themselves which otherwise would be swamped out. This effect is enhanced by simultaneously listening to "pink noise" on earphones. A primitive ganzfeld device is to place a half Ping-Pong ball over each eye to give a uniform featureless light field. Commercially produced more advanced ganzfeld devices are available. The RAS also 'switches on' the cortex during the sensory deprivation of sleep; visions occur (dreams), but as the brain's awareness level in sleep is very low (no beta waves), these dreams cannot be manipulated. Electronic units described in Chapter 9, are designed to overcome this and convert the dream to lucid. Meditation while we are awake is the manipulation of the RAS to create reverie and higher states of consciousness, with awareness. Floating in an isolation tank has a strong effect on the RAS, causing deep relaxation combined with great alertness - a very unusual state. The sensory deprivation caused by the tank causes the RAS to 'turn up the volume' on all the senses, bringing even the involuntary functions like heartbeat under conscious control, thereby achieving a unity between the reptile brain (RAS), limbic system (autonomic system) and neocortex (conscious awareness and voluntary control) (41). After some time, subliminal visions may begin to present themselves.

Hutchison (41) points out that paradoxically, the RAS also interprets the experience of floating as a type of sensory overload on some channels and so responds by causing deep relaxation. Hence the unique result of floating is deep relaxation with intense conscious awareness.

Floating also causes the limbic system to inhibit stress hormones such as epinephrine and adrenaline, while increasing the production of endorphins which are beneficial neurochemicals. This results in a reduction of anxiety and induces euphoria, and helps the cortex to synchronise its hemispheres, to generate theta waves and visualise, etc. Habitual, chronic stress has replaced earlier primitive threats like loss of life, territorial combat and starvation, and modern man is in a perpetual state of non-specific arousal (128). Many experts consider about 85% of all illness is stress-related. In the flotation tank there is sanctuary from stress situations: there are no other people, no noise, no light, and nothing that needs doing; in this absence of threats, body chemicals return to (better than) normal and one has the chance to examine one's life calmly and objectively.

Tank treatment is not passive but has an equal and opposite effect to what any stress could have. Hutchison (41) points out that our Judeo-Christian ethos imbues a tendency to regard relaxation as something opposed to productive activity: if you're relaxed this means you're not performing any worthwhile activity! Its apparent wasting time and laziness aspects makes it appear to be a luxury.

The limbic system atop the brain stem is responsible for some effects of altered states of consciousness such as euphoria, feelings of divided consciousness, loss of awareness of body boundaries, feelings of floating or flying and strange visual experiences like white or golden light (5).

Most people have been taught to avoid solitude, isolation & confinement. TV sets are anti-isolation devices. So most people have a negative attitude to solitude & isolation (6). It is thus necessary to make a (small) mental effort to overcome this feeling.

In Summary, the benefits of flotation are:

• Floating stimulates endorphin production, described under CES, in Chapter 11. It quickly & considerably reduces stress & anxiety and reduces any tendency for heart disease and other stress-related illnesses by lowering the levels of stress-related biochemicals.

• Floating immediately brings forward the right brain hemisphere, giving unusual access to imagination, creativity, visualisation and problem solving.

• It allows remarkable "superlearning", verified and used by many universities & schools mainly in the USA. Tape recorded and video information is accurately assimilated.

- Two hours of floating are more restorative than a full night of sound sleep and the deepest rest ever experienced is attained.

- Athletes improve performance using flotation.

- Floating quickly reduces smoking and drug use and counteracts withdrawal symptoms (by raising endorphin production).

- Floating is effective if weight loss is desired and its effect lasts for months after floating.

- Dogmatic attitudes and beliefs are realised for what they are, while floating. Unreasonable resistance to new ideas is thus weakened - a very beneficial effect.

CHAPTER 11

OTHER MACHINES

Some other machines have been recently reviewed (2). To mention a few, there is the TENS unit which gives very low voltage and current stimulation to the ankles at about 8 Hz, reported to produce interesting perceptual results; the Graham potentializer is more complex but again is reported to give very interesting effects.

Cranial Electrical Stimulator (CES)

This is a remarkable electronic unit.

Although there have been no reported problems or significant side effects, these units are not recommended for people with epilepsy, persons with heart trouble or pacemakers, or persons who have had a recent stroke.

Cranial Electrical Stimulation (CES) was developed in the USSR in the late 1940s and has been widely used. Research shows that CES produces a mild stimulation of the hypothalamic area of the brain, balancing neurotransmitter activity, in particular beta endorphin & norepinephrine. The effects are like the so called "jogger's high"; habitual joggers experience a slightly euphoric state due to endorphin production and experience 'withdrawal' symptoms if they miss jogging sessions. A CES machine can remove these withdrawal symptoms, and, can also remove withdrawal symptoms experienced by drug abuse. CES is a powerful way for treatment of drug abuse. Narcotic drugs replace the body's natural opiates (endorphins) and the body stops making them, and if the drugs are then stopped the body still doesn't make them and the user gets the awful withdrawal symptoms which we normally do not experience because we have our natural 'opiates' in our systems to protect us from such an effect. If we had no natural endorphins, we would all have awful 'withdrawal symptoms' all the time!

Use of CES devices may cause interesting occurrences of vivid dreams; see the section below on the Dream Machine for some explanation.

High quality CES devices use a 3-wire output, which gives dual frequency capability, producing two simultaneous brainwave states. Some units may use only two wires and can thus apparently only give one frequency.

Two independently settable frequencies will also give a third frequency by interference or beat. Fortuitously, beta minus alpha = theta (e.g. 17 - 11 = 6).

CES units are very simple to use: the stimulus pads are connected to your ear lobes and back of neck. Very low currents are used, in the microamp region (cf the milliamps of the TENS machines used routinely medically for intractable pain relief). Battery operation is essential for complete electrical safety: no mains connections.

CES units enhance endorphin production which assists in reaching deep levels of relaxation.

Neuroscientific studies have shown dramatic improvements in the following areas:
deep relaxation, improved memory, mental clarity, improved learning, mood elevation, sound sleep, increased vitality, increased concentration, reduction of psychosomatic conditions, alternative to addictive substances.

Some CES units can be synchronised with the flickering lights of light & sound machines.

A remarkable well-established machine called the Braintuner, is a cranial electrical stimulator (CES) which simultaneously generates 256 different beneficial frequencies applied conveniently to the earlobes (similarly to the above unit). Based on previous machines going back several decades, this unit is a major advance in CES. Its uses include placing the user at the alpha/theta border (Schumann frequency, 7.83 Hz, matching the Earth's electromagnetic resonance frequency), gaining insight, remarkably effective release from drug addiction, TENS-type pain relief usages (relieving intractable pain - on medical advice to do so, of course), insomnia relief, etc..

CES units allow the user to quickly learn how to get into advanced meditation states (compare 10 years by conventional meditation methods).

They promote brain hemisphere balance, between logical and intuitive abilities. This balance can improve communicative skills and creative thinking. Out-of-the-body experiences and other psychic effects have been reported by users. Many users report reduced sleep requirement, about 2 hours per night less than before use. Excellent results are reported when used with language tapes etc.

The pulse wave is advantageously buffered with a complex waveform to make it more effective. Frequency is user variable usually from about 0.5 to 14 Hz. The intensity is adjustable usually from 5 to 50 microamps, well below the limits set by the FDA (USA).

CES units can benefit:
students who wish to improve concentration,
musicians and artists who want to enhance creativity,
business people who wish to reduce stress & improve managerial skills,
meditation students who want to enter advanced states of consciousness,
athletes who want to enhance mental strength, improving performance,
psychotherapists,
and anyone who wishes to explore their mind and approach life in a relaxed way.

They can be used with language tapes, meditation tapes, subliminal tapes, and music. They enhance mental and physical relaxation and so allow self-improvement regimes to work more effectively.

CES units intended for the medical treatment of anxiety, depression & drug addiction usually operate at a fixed frequency of 100 Hz and so will not interrupt normal activities and can be used while reading, typing, etc. (It should not be used while operating machinery). It is reported to release endorphins and to have the consequent beneficial effects.

Budzynski (133) has published a review on CES and Beck (134) has given a list of published papers on CES.

Ganzfeld Units

First discovered in the 1930s by psychologists, a featureless uniform white or coloured (but not black) visual field can cause the brain to "shift gear" into profound meditation states. Ganzfeld is german for "entire field" (of view).

A ganzfeld unit presents a steady (non-pulsing), luminous but featureless visual field to the eyes, which causes relaxation, gives stress relief and brings forward imagery which is normally blotted out by the wealth and variety of all the normal objects which we see in any room. Removing all such normal objects causes the brain to "turn up the gain control" (analogous to brightness control on a TV) which allows normally-too-faint images to appear. If random noise is gently played through earphones, the effect is enhanced. Merely closing the eyes (featureless dark field) does not produce these results.

Gazing into a ganzfeld, the mind eventually 'blanks out'; you do not see blankness but instead lose the sensation of having eyes at all. One's attention then turns within and deeply relaxed meditative states are entered.

Dream Machines

You can enjoy the power of being awake and aware in your dreams!

These remarkable units answer the wishes of people for centuries - a way of entering their dreams with self-conscious awareness and taking part in them (called lucid dreams). This extends your conscious time from day into the night and many useful experiences can be gained which have a direct bearing on one's everyday life. Up till recently, this possibility was only "in the compass of a dream...", but is now a reality! In dreaming sleep, rapid eye movements (REM) occur (81) and by using a sensitive electronic sensor this event can by sent to a microprocessor unit which then sends a train of low-level flashes to a subminiature lamp set into a light-shield worn by the sleeper. The light-shield is similar to those which airlines give out on night flights, for passengers who want to sleep in a lit cabin. When the unit detects REM, indicating dreaming sleep, and responds thus, the dreamer sees the dream light up, or some other event occurs, like bright jewels suddenly appearing. The effect of this is to trigger the memory of having set up the experiment to become aware and self-conscious in the dream! At that instant the dream suddenly becomes much more vivid or lucid and one can take conscious part in directing it. It forms a remarkable experience.

You can find out how it feels to fly, to climb the highest mountain, to visit exotic lands; you can use lucid dreaming to help you make your dreams come true in real-life. Throughout history, dreams have inspired many great new ideas and inventions. With lucid dreaming you can go directly to the source of inspiration within your unconscious mind to stimulate ideas and solve problems.

Lucid dreams are so real that you can use them to practice and improve skills. Lucid dreamers have thus developed their techniques in sports, dancing, music, speaking, mathematics, science, surgery, computer programming, etc. etc. Fears can be overcome. Your conscious and unconscious minds can be brought together which helps you to grow psychologically. Lucid dreaming is especially valuable for those interested in dreams as a path to self-knowledge.

Because of the complexity of design of a unit which will reliably perform this function without needing continual adjustments, the price of these units is unavoidably high. But the value for money is there. The units are the product of years of dream research at various institutes. They have been well tested by many people with great success.

Normally, people have about 5 or more dreams in an 8-hour sleep period, but forget most of them on waking. One is not normally aware or self-conscious in dreams because the brain is not in a beta brainwave-producing state. For some awareness, some beta waves must be produced, along with the predominantly theta waves of the dream state. This is the function of these units.

Some more details were given earlier, at the end of Chapter 9.

CONCLUSION

It may be significant that some of the techniques described in this book are very simple and can be performed with readily available equipment that is easy to use.

The acceptance of these techniques by major organisations in the USA is now spreading to Europe and a new era where subconscious enhancement and the ability to tap into our inner being is beginning.

Many of the electronic units and other devices, such as flotation tanks, are available from CMC Ltd, 25 Lexham Garden, London W8 5JJ [Tel 071-581-9919; Fax 071-225-8712]. A free catalogue is available.

A basic reading list of classic books which give a major contribution in this whole field and related fields is as follows:

Key references (not in order of importance):
1,2,**4**,**5**,**6**,**7**,8,**11**,14,15,**16**,17,**20**,21,**23**,24,26,31,33,34,38,4 1,43,**47**,48,**84**, 89,90, **91**,92,**95**-105,111,114,115.

In conclusion, with the help of these new electronic units we can all at least aspire towards becoming Einsteins or to writing rhymes of ancient mariners, or composing music and painting masterpieces, or producing inspired films and videos: Tolkein's 'Middle Earth', Lewis Carrol's 'looking glass', C.S.Lewis's 'Narnia', the 'Fantasia' of The Neverending Story and the magical world of A Flight of Dragons (26). None (and all!) of these are "children's videos"!

Concentration - Meditation - Contemplation
Dharana   -   Dhyana   -   Samadhi

REFERENCES

1. A. Huxley, "The Doors of Perception" , Penguin, (1960). .
2. M. Hutchison, "Megabrain", Morrow, NY (1986)
3. W. Grey Walter, "The Living Brain", Pelican (1961).
4. E & A Green, "Beyond Biofeedback", Delacorte Press, USA, (1977). Also see Research Centre J. (T.S.), 16, no 4, p 87 (1972).
5. C. Maxwell Cade & N. Coxhead, "The Awakened Mind", Element Books, UK, (1989). &
   G.G. Blundell, C. Maxwell Cade, "EEG Measurement", Published by Audio Ltd, London.
6. J. C. Lilley, "In the centre of the Cyclone", Paladin (1973).
7. R. A. Monroe, "Journeys out of the Body", Anchor (1977).
8. O. Fox, "Astral Projection", University Books, NY, USA (1962) & Citadel Press, NJ.
9. Yram, "Practical Astral Projection", S. Weiser, New York, (1979).

10. B. Steiger, "Astral Projection", Para Research Inc., Rockport, MA (1982).
11. J. H. Brennan, "Astral Doorways", Aquarian Press (1971).
12. N. R. Clough, "How to make and use magic Mirrors", Aquarian Press (1977).
13. W. Sargant, "Battle for the Mind", Great Pan (1957).
14. M. Sadhu, "Concentration", Unwin Paperbacks (1977).
15. H. Hewitt, "Meditation", Teach Yourself Books, Hodder & Stoughton (1978).
16. A. E. , "The Candle of Vision" , University Books Inc. NY.
17. R. M. Bucke, "Cosmic Consciousness", Dutton, USA, (1969).
18. J. Silva & P. Miele, "The Silva mind control method", Souvenir Press (1978).
19. G. I. Gurdjieff, "Views from the Real World", Routledge & Kegen
20. C. Castaneda, "The Teachings of Don Juan", (& other titles), Penguin (1977).
21. Paramhansa Yogananda, "Autobiography of a Yogi" , Rider, London (1961).
22. Maharishi Mahesh Yogi, "Commentary on the Bhagavad Gita", Penguin (1969).
23. "Highways of the Mind", "The Shining Paths", "Inner Landscapes" and other books by D Ashcroft-Nowicki, Aquarian Press (1980s).
24. Translations of books by F.Lefebure (list avail. from Psychotec Publ, 5 Haig Lane, Church Crookham, Fleet, GU13 0UN.) Some titles are:
"Brain development by alternative audition" by Dr F.Lefebure (Psychotechnic Publications, 5 Haig Lane, Church Crookham, Fleet, GU13 OUN, UK) [english translation of book below]
"L'activation du cerveau par l'audition alternative (alternophonie)" by Dr F.Lefebure (Editions Jacques Bersez, Paris)
"Phosphenism - the art of visualization" by Dr F.Lefebure (Psychotechnic Publi cations, 5 Haig Lane, Church Crookham, Fleet, GU13 OUN, UK) [english translation]
"Developing clairvoyance by phosphenism" by Dr F.Lefebure (Psychotechnic Publi cations, 5 Haig Lane, Church Crookham, Fleet, GU13 OUN, UK)
"L'exploration du cerveau par les oscillations des phosphenes

doubles (phosphe nisme)" by Dr F.Lefebure (Editions Jacques Bersez, Paris, 1982)

"Du moulin a priere a la dynamo spirituelle (Kundalini)" by Dr F.Lefebure (Editions Jacques Bersez, Paris, 1982)

"Le pneumophene (phosphenisme)" by Dr F.Lefebure (Editions Jacques Bersez, Paris, 1982)

[Translations of some of these are also available from The SEED Institute, 10 Magnolia Way, Fleet, GU19 9JZ, UK]

25. J. Vernon , "Inside the Black Room", C. N. Potter Inc., New York, (1963).

26. VIDEOS: "The Lion, Witch & Wardrobe" (cartoon version, Vestron CAD 14194); "The Neverending Story"; "A Flight of Dragons" (Channel 5, CFV05732); these are just a few highly recommended examples.

27. L.E. Walkup, Perceptual Motor Skills 21, 35-41 (1965).

28. R. May, "Creativity & its cultivation", ed. H.B.Anderson, Harper & Bros., NY, (1959).

29. A. Kasamatsu & T. Hirai, Psychologia, 6, 86-91 (1963).

30. VIDEO: Koyaanisqatsi (Polygram Video Ltd, 083 448 3).

31. "Auditory beats in the brain", Scientific American, 94-102, (October 1973)/32. C. Green , "Lucid Dreams", (Inst of

32. Psychphysical Research, Oxford, 1968)

33. K. Harary & P. Weintraub, "Lucid Dreams in 30 Days", Aquarian Press (1989)

34. K. Harary & P. Weintraub, "An Out-of-the-Body Experience in 30 Days", Aquarian Press, 1989)

35. H.de Saint-Denys, "Dreams & How to guide them", Duckworth, London, (1982)

36. M. Watkins, "Waking Dreams", Spring Publ.Inc, Dallas (1984)

37. S.J. Blackmore, "Beyond the Body", Paladin (1986)

38. J.H. Brennan, "Discover Astral Projection", Aquarian/Thorsons (1991)

39. S. Muldoon & H. Carrington, "Projection of the Astral Body", Rider (1958)

40. C. Green, "Out of the Body Experiences", Inst for Psychophysical Research, Oxford (1968)

41. M. Hutchison , "The Book of Floating", Quill - Morrow, New York

(1984)
42. The Book of Ecclesiastes
43. Michael S Gazzaniga "The Split Brain in Man", Scientific American, 24-29, Oct. 1967.
44. S. Rose, "The making of memory", Bantam (1992)
45. F.C. Happold, "Mysticism" (1963)
46. C. Tart, "Altered States of Consciousness" (Wiley, NY, 1969)
47. E.C. Steinbecher, "Inner Guide Meditation", Aquarian Press, UK (1988)
48. M. Zdenek, "The Right-brain Experience", Corgi (1983)
49. Megabrain Report, 1990
50. O. Simonton et al, "Getting well again", Tarcher, Los Angeles (1978)
51. M. Westcott & J. Ranzoni, "Correlates of Intuitive Thinking", Psychological Reports, 12, 595-613 (1963).
52. R.L. Walford, "Maximum Life Span", Norton, NY (1983)
53. G. Leonard, "The Silent Pulse", Dutton, NY (1978)
54. P.H.C. Mutke, "Selective Awareness", Celestial Arts, Millbrae, CA (1976)
55. R.D. Willard, Am J Clin Hypnos 19, 195 (1977)
56. J.E. Williams, J Sex Res 10, 316-24 (1974)
57. J. Hooper, "Interview with C. Pert", Omni, (Feb. 1982)
58. G Rattray Taylor, "The Natural History of the Mind", Dutton, NY (1979)
59. P.B. Applewhite, "Molecular Gods: how molecules determine our behaviour" Prentice-Hall (1981)
60. J. Olds, Scientific American 195, 105-116 (1956)
61. J. Olds, Am Psychologist 24, 707-719 (1969)
62. J.E. Adam, Pain 2, 161-6 (1976)
63. J.B. Levine et al, Nature 272, 826-7 (1978)
64. D.J. Mayer et al, Brain Res 121, 360-73 (1977)
65. H. Benson & R.K. Wallace, "Decreased drug abuse with Transcendental Meditation: A study of 1862 subjects", Congressional Record, 92nd Congress, 1st Session, June 1971.
66. M. Shafii et al, Am J Psychiatry 131, 60-3 (1975)
67. Idem, ibid 132, 942-5 (1975)
68. Time, 19 Jan 1981

69. M.Csikszentmihalyi, "Beyond boredom & anxiety", Jossey-Bass, San Francisco & London (1975)
70. P.D. MacLean, "A triune concept of the brain & behaviour", Univ of Toronto Press (1973)
71. "How the brain works", Newsweek, 7 Feb 1983
72. J.C. Lilly, "The deep self", Simon & Schuster, NY (1977)
73. H. Benson, "The Relaxation Response", Morrow, NY (1975).
74. T. Budzynski, Proc First Intl Conf on R.E.S.T. & Self-regulation, Denver, CO, (18 March, 1983)
75. Alan Richardson, "Mental Imagery", Springer-Verlag, NY (1969).
76. B.C. Glueck & C.F. Stroebel, Comprehensive Psychiatry 16, 303-21 (1975)
77. J.P. Banquet, J Electroencephalography & Clin Neurophysiol 33, 449-58 (1972)
78. Idem, ibid 35, 143-51 (1973)
79. J.W. Turner, Proc First Intl Conf on R.E.S.T. & Self-regulation (Denver, CO, 18 March, 1983)
80. Diana Deutsch, "Musical Illusions", Scientific American, 92-104, Oct (1975).
81. Nathaniel Kleitman, "Patterns of Dreaming" Sceintific American, 82-88, Nov. (1960).
82. S.Ostrander & L.Schroeder, "Superlearning", Delacorte Press, NY (1979)
83. G.Lozanov, "Suggestology & outlines of suggestopedy", Gordon & Breach, (1982)
84. N. Drury, "Music for Inner Space", Prism Press, UK (1985)
85. A. Puharich, "The sacred mushroom", Doubleday (1959)
86. "Beyond Telepathy" idem, Doubleday (1962)
87. J. Dunlap, "Exploring inner space", Harcourt Brace & World (1961)
88. D. Solomon, "LSD, the consciousness-expanding drug", Putnam, London (1964)
89. "Drug Experience" ed. by D. Ebin (Orion Press)
90. Lama Anagarika , "The Way of the White Clouds" Govinda Rider (1966)
91. I.Tweedie "The Chasm of Fire", Element Books, UK (1979)
92. Gopi Krishna, "Kundalini", Robinson & Watkins (1971)

93. "The secret of Yoga" idem, Turnstone Books, London (1972)
94. Mouni Sadhu, "Samadhi", Allen & Unwin (1962)
95. Dr R.A. Moody, "Life After Life", Bantam Books, (1977) (a best seller)
96. Dr R.A. Moody, "Reflections on Life After Life", Bantam Books.
97. H.Wambach, "Life Before Life", Bantam (1981)
98. Dr M.B.Sabom , "Recollections of Death", Corgi, UK (1982)
99. D.Scott Rogo, "The return from silence", Aquarian Press, (1981) and "Life after death" idem, Harper-Collins, Glasgow, (1992)
100. P. Lemesurier, "The Great Pyramid decoded", Element Books (1977)
101. Suzuki, "Zen mind & beginner's mind", (& other titles), Weatherhill, NY, (1970)
102. E. Herrigel, "Zen in the Art of Archery", Routlege & Kegan Paul
103. Z'ev ben Shimon Halevi (Warren Kenton), "Kabbalah", Thames & Hudson, London (1979)
104. S. Court, "The meditator's manual", Aquarian Press, UK (1984)
105. P. Russell, "Meditation", published by BBC, London (1979)
106. D. & J. Beck, "The pleasure connexion: how endorphins affect our health & happiness".
107. "Altered States of Consciousness" ed. by C.P. Tart (1990)
108. M. Csikszentmihalyi, "Flow: the psychology of optimal experience".
109. P. Kelder, "Tibetan secrets of youth & vitality", Harper Collins, Glasgow (1991)
110. Graham Greene, "A World of my own: a Dream Diary", Reinhardt (1992).
111. P. Brunton, "In search of secret Egypt" (& other books).
112. R.O. Becker & G. Selden, "The body electric" and R.O.Becker, "Cross currents".
113. C.W. Leadbeater, "The Chakras", Theos Publ House, London.
114. Patanjali, "Yoga Aphorisms".
115. M.G. Hocking, "ESP observation of atoms & molecules", Bull Theo Sci Stdy Gp 21, 53 (1983) & 22, 5 (1984) [reprints available from the author at 2 Boxgrove Road, Guildford GU1 2LX].
116. Dr Joel Funk, Professor of Psychology, Plymouth State College,

New Hampshire.

117. Nature <u>345</u>, 463 (1990)
118. Science News <u>137</u>, 229 (1990)
119. The Lancet, Jan 1983, p.246
120. New England J Medicine <u>307</u>, 249 (1982)
121. New Yorker, 12 June 1989, p.69
122. Cancer Research Aug 1988, p.4222
123. E. Swedenborg, "Heaven & its wonders and hell", (Swedenborg Foundation, New York; distributed by Popular Library, New York, 1960)
124."Neurochemical responses to CES & photo-stimulation via brainwave synchronization" study by Dr R.K. Cady & Dr N. Shealy at Shealy Institute of Comprehensive health care, Springfield, Missouri (1990), 11 pages
125. A. Koestler, "The act of creation", Pan Books, London (1984)
126. B. Edwards, "Drawing on the Right Side of the Brain".
127. Doreen Kimura, "The Asymmetry of the Human Brain", Scientific American, 70-78 (1973).
128. K. R. Pelletier, "Mind as Healer, Mind as Slayer", Derlacorte Press, NY (1977).
129.G. Oster, 'Auditory Beats in the Brain', Scientific American <u>229</u>, 94-102   (1973)].
130. A.R. Luria, article in "Recent Progress in Perception" publ. Freeman, San   Francisco (1970).
131. F.H. Atwater, Hemi-Sync Journal, <u>11</u>, No 1 (1993)
132. F.J. Boersma & C. Gagnon, Medical Hypnoanalysis Journal <u>7</u> (3), 80-97 (1992)].
133.T.H. Budzynski, "Cranial Electrical Stimulation (CES) and the Practitioner" (publ. by CES Labs., 14770 N.E. 95th, Redmond, WA 98052, USA.)
134. R. Beck, "Bibliography of Cranial Electro-Stimulation" (publ. by Allied Forces Inc., PO Box 1530, Stanwood, WA 98292, USA.)
135.I. Wickramsekera, "Sensory Restriction and Self-Hypnosis as Potentiators of Self Refulation." Paper delivered at First International Conference on REST and Self-Refulation, Denver, Colorado, March 18, (1983).

136. "Restricted Environmental Stimulation & the Enhancement of Hypnotizability: Pain, EEg Alpha, Skin Conductance and Temperature Responses,", The International Journal of Clinical and Experimental Hypnosis, Vol. 2, 147-166 (1982).

NOTICE: For legal reasons we make the following statements. The items in described in this book are experimental consciousness-enhancing products, for which no medical claims are made or implied. The descriptions given for each product are reports of the effects produced as given by the manufacturers and by professional users. None of these statements by professionals should be construed as medical claims. The claims made centre around relaxation, meditation, hypnosis and learning.

Warning: Light & sound and CES units should not be used by persons with a history of epilepsy or other neurological disorders. But the following finding is quoted, for information, from Maxwell Cade & Coxhead (5): "After 4 years use of the lights, with more than 4000 pupils including 25 known epileptics, there have been no mishaps, and most of the epileptics have reported a marked improvement in their condition. ...subjects were only exposed to the lights after they had become very relaxed..." (see page 49 in reference 5 for more details). This is quoted for information only and our advice is that medical advice should be obtained before proceeding in such cases.

Additionally, it is sensible to allow half an hour after using light and sound machines and other mind-enhancing units and tapes before operating machinery or driving a car.